Active Experiences for Active Children

MATHEMATICS

Carol Seefeldt
Institute for Child Study
University of Maryland, College Park

Alice Galper
Curriculum and Instruction
University of Maryland, College Park

Upper Saddle River, New Jersey
Columbus, Ohio

L.C.C. SOUTH CAMPUS LIBRARY

Library of Congress Cataloging in Publication Data

Seefeldt, Carol.
    Active experiences for active children: mathematics / Carol Seefeldt, Alice Galper.
      p. cm.
    Includes bibliographical references and index.
    ISBN 0-13-083434-3 (pbk.)
      1. Mathematics—Study and teaching (Early childhood)—Activity programs. I. Galper, Alice. II. Title.

QA 135.6.S44 2004
372.7—dc21

2002037852

Vice President and Executive Publisher: Jeffery W. Johnston
Publisher: Kevin M. Davis
Associate Editor: Christina M. Tawney
Editorial Assistant: Autumn Crisp
Production Editor: Sheryl Glicker Langner
Design Coordinator: Diane C. Lorenzo
Photo Coordinator: Sandy Schaefer
Cover Designer: Debra Warrenfeltz
Cover photo: Getty Images
Production Manager: Laura Messerly
Director of Marketing: Ann Castel Davis
Marketing Manager: Amy June
Marketing Coordinator: Tyra Poole

QA
135.6
.S44
2004

This book was set in Times and Frutiger by Carlisle Communications, Ltd. It was printed and bound by Courier Kendallville, Inc. The cover was printed by Phoenix Color Corp.

Photo Credits: pp. 3, 69 by Karen Mancinelli/Pearson Learning; pp. 13, 72 by Scott Cunningham/Merrill; pp. 29, 51, 134 by Anne Vega/Merrill; pp. 39, 85, 127 by Barbara Schwartz/Merrill; p. 57 by Valerie Schultz/Merrill; p. 88 by Paul S. Conklin/PhotoEdit; p. 99 by Laima Druskis/PH College; p. 106 by Roy Ramsey/PH College; pp. 115, 120 by Anthony Magnacca/Merrill.

Copyright © 2004 by Pearson Education, Inc., Upper Saddle River, New Jersey 07458.
Pearson Prentice Hall. All rights reserved. Printed in the United States of America. This publication is protected by Copyright and permission should be obtained from the publisher prior to any prohibited reproduction, storage in a retrieval system, or transmission in any form or by any means, electronic, mechanical, photocopying, recording, or likewise. For information regarding permission(s), write to: Rights and Permissions Department.

Pearson Prentice Hall™ is a trademark of Pearson Education, Inc.
Pearson® is a registered trademark of Pearson plc
Prentice Hall® is a registered trademark of Pearson Education, Inc.
Merrill® is a registered trademark of Pearson Education, Inc.

Pearson Education Ltd.
Pearson Education Singapore Pte. Ltd.
Pearson Education Canada, Ltd.
Pearson Education—Japan

Pearson Education Australia Pty. Limited
Pearson Education North Asia Ltd.
Pearson Educación de Mexico, S.A. de C.V.
Pearson Education Malaysia Pte. Ltd.

10 9 8 7 6 5 4 3 2 1
ISBN: 0-13-083434-3

Preface

"What can I do tomorrow?" teachers ask. "I've run out of ideas. And I don't mean just another silly activity. I need something that will keep children involved and lead to successful learning." Grounded in John Dewey's philosophy that all genuine education comes through experience, but that not all experiences are equally educative, *Active Experiences for Active Children: Mathematics* answers teachers' questions about what to do tomorrow and on into the school year. The book is also based on the theory that children construct their own meaning from active encounters with their environment and through the support of adults and more accomplished peers.

Both pre- and in-service teachers will find this book useful. It is suitable as a text, or a supplemental text, for early childhood courses in community colleges and four-year college programs. The experiences in this book would provide a basis for a series of workshops or short courses in mathematics for children.

There are numerous activity books available. These, however, present isolated math activities that are often meaningless to children and void of any real content or learning. *Active Experiences for Active Children: Mathematics* offers teachers an integrated approach to planning mathematics learning for young children.

Its practicality will also be ideal for teachers who desire the best for young children but have limited training or formal preparation for teaching mathematics. Professionals working in childcare, Head Start, or other early childhood settings will find that *Active Experiences for Active Children: Mathematics* supports their growth and understanding of how to put theory into practice.

ORGANIZATION

This book is the fourth in a series of books designed to illustrate how to plan and implement meaningful, thematic experiences that truly educate young children instead of just keeping them busy. Teachers are given guides to planning and implementing curriculum that will lead to children's academic success using developmentally appropriate methods for teaching mathematics. Experiences conform to the standards of the National Council of Teachers of Mathematics and the National Association for the Education of Young Children.

Active Experiences for Active Children: Mathematics consists of clear, concise, and usable guides for planning meaningful mathematics content and teaching strategies for children in childcare, preschool, Head Start, or other early educational programs. Experiences are expanded into the primary grades.

The experiences in this book lead to successful mathematics learning because they

- are grounded in children's interests and needs in their here-and-now world
- have integrity in terms of content key to mathematics learning

- involve children in group work, investigations, and projects
- have continuity. One experience builds on another, forming a complete, coherent, integrated learning curriculum for young children as well as connecting the early childhood setting to children's homes and communities.
- provide time and opportunity for children to think and reflect on their experiences
- contain a large number of resources (books, Web sites, magazines, audios, and visuals) for both teachers and children

The first four chapters describe the foundation for planning and implementing experiential mathematics learning. These offer pre- and in-service teachers of young children an overview of theory and research based upon Dewey, the constructivist view of children's learning, and the latest guidelines proposed for the mathematics curriculum. The first chapter illustrates how theories of learning and teaching can be put into practice. This is followed by a chapter on indoor and outdoor environments for mathematics. Next the book considers the importance of building home-school connections for math learning. Finally, chapter 4 reviews research and theory and discusses mathematics content, methodology, and teaching strategies.

Next, chapters based upon content suggested by the National Association of Teachers of Mathematics and the National Association for the Education of Young Children are presented. There are six experiences based upon the content areas. These guides include sections for the teacher and for the children.

The section "For the Teacher" begins by identifying concepts key to learning mathematics. Goals and objectives are stated. This section discusses concrete ideas for connecting children's home and family to the school, and describes how to evaluate and assess children's mathematics learning.

The section "For the Children" consists of ideas for implementing the identified goals and objectives through thematic, integrated, and continual experiences. In this case, the guides are based on knowledge, skills, resources, and environments required for children to construct mathematics concepts.

AUTHORS

Another important feature of the book is the expertise and background of the authors. Together, they bring a unique perspective to the book. Both have experienced Deweyan education. Both have worked in Head Start, childcare, and other early childhood settings and thus bring an intimate knowledge of practice to the text. And because both are researchers, the latest in theory and research in the field of early childhood education is represented in the text.

ACKNOWLEDGMENTS

We would like to thank our editors and the following reviewers: Thomasenia Lott Adams, University of Florida; Cecelia Benelli, Western Illinois University; Diane Cerreto, Eastern Connecticut State University; Karen Colleran, Pierce College; and Christine Nucci, Arizona State University, West.

Discover the Companion Website Accompanying This Book

The Prentice Hall Companion Website: A Virtual Learning Environment

Technology is a constantly growing and changing aspect of our field that is creating a need for content and resources. To address this emerging need, Prentice Hall has developed an online learning environment for students and professors alike—Companion Websites—to support our textbooks.

In creating a Companion Website, our goal is to build on and enhance what the textbook already offers. For this reason, the content for each user-friendly website is orga-nized by topic and provides the professor and student with a variety of meaningful resources. Common features of a Companion Website include:

For the Professor—

Every Companion Website integrates **Syllabus Manager**™, an online syllabus creation and management utility.

- **Syllabus Manager**™ provides you, the instructor, with an easy, step-by-step process to create and revise syllabi, with direct links into Companion Website and other online content without having to learn HTML.

- Students may logon to your syllabus during any study session. All they need to know is the web address for the Companion Website and the password you've assigned to your syllabus.

- After you have created a syllabus using **Syllabus Manager**™, students may enter the syllabus for their course section from any point in the Companion Website.

- Clicking on a date, the student is shown the list of activities for the assignment. The activities for each assignment are linked directly to actual content, saving time for students.

- Adding assignments consists of clicking on the desired due date, then filling in the details of the assignment—name of the assignment, instructions, and whether or not it is a one-time or repeating assignment.

- In addition, links to other activities can be created easily. If the activity is online, a URL can be entered in the space provided, and it will be linked automatically in the final syllabus.

- Your completed syllabus is hosted on our servers, allowing convenient updates from any computer on the Internet. Changes you make to your syllabus are immediately available to your students at their next logon.

For the Student—

- **Introduction**—General information about the topic and how it will be covered in the website.
- **Web Links**—A variety of websites related to topic areas.
- **Timely Articles**—Links to online articles that enable you to become more aware of important issues in early childhood.
- **Learn by Doing**—Put concepts into action, participate in activities, examine strategies, and more.
- **Visit a School**—Visit a school's website to see concepts, theories, and strategies in action.
- **For Teachers/Practitioners**—Access information you will need to know as an educator, including information on materials, activities, and lessons.
- **Current Policies and Standards**—Find out the latest early childhood policies from the government and various organizations, and view state, federal, and curriculum standards.
- **Resources and Organizations**—Discover tools to help you plan your classroom or center and organizations to provide current information and standards for each topic.
- **Electronic Bluebook**—Paperless method of completing homework or essays assigned by a professor. Finished work can be sent to the professor via email.
- **Message Board**—Virtual bulletin board to post and respond to questions and comments from a national audience.

To take advantage of these and other resources, please visit the *Active Experiences for Active Children: Mathematics* Companion Website at

www.prenhall.com/seefeldt

About the Authors

Carol Seefeldt, Ph.D., is Professor Emeritus of human development at the Institute for Child Study, University of Maryland, College Park, where she continues to teach graduate and undergraduate classes. She received the Distinguished Scholar-Researcher award from the university and has published 25 books and over 100 scholarly and research articles for teachers and parents. Her books include *Social Studies for the Preschool/Primary Child, Active Experiences for Active Children: Literacy Emerges,* and *Current Issues in Early Childhood Education* (all with Alice Galper). She has also written *Playing to Learn* and *Creating Rooms of Wonder.* She coauthored *Early Childhood: Where Learning Begins—Geography* for the U.S. Department of Education.

During her 40 years in the field, Dr. Seefeldt has taught at every level from nursery school for 2-year-olds through third grade. In Florida, she directed a church-related kindergarten, and served as Regional Training Officer for Project Head Start. She has frequently conducted teacher-training programs in the United States, Japan, and Ukraine, and is a frequent guest on radio and television talk shows.

Carol's research has revolved around program development and evaluation. She pioneered the study of intergenerational attitudes, and was the director of the Montgomery County Head Start—Public School Transition Demonstration Evaluation.

Alice Galper, Ph. D., educator and consultant, received her doctorate from the University of Maryland, College Park. Previously, she was a classroom teacher in New Hampshire and a Head Start Consultant in the Washington, D.C., area. She was a professor of human development teaching graduate and undergraduate courses in early childhood and human development at Mt. Vernon College, Washington, D.C., for nearly 20 years and at the University of Maryland. She assisted Carol Seefeldt on the research component of the Montgomery County Head Start—Public School Transition Demonstration Evaluation. Currently she is on the adjunct faculty at the University of Maryland.

Alice's research has revolved around intergenerational attitudes and program evaluation. She has written many articles for such journals as *Child Development, Journal of Educational Psychology,* and *Early Childhood Research Quarterly.*

Alice presents workshops and papers regularly at the National Association for the Education of Young Children Conference, the Head Start Research Conference, and the Society for Research in Child Development Biennial Meetings, among others.

Active in community affairs, Alice has been appointed by Mayor Anthony Williams of Washington, D.C., as cochair of the Interagency Coordinating Council of the DC Early Intervention Program for Infants and Toddlers, and she volunteers for Mary's Center for Maternal and Child Care, Inc.

THE EASIEST WAY TO ENHANCE YOUR COURSE
Proven Journals • Proven Strategies • Proven Media

www.EducatorLearningCenter.com

Merrill Education is pleased to announce a new partnership with ASCD. The result of this partnership is a joint website, www.EducatorLearningCenter.com, with recent articles and cutting-edge teaching strategies. The Educator Learning Center combines the resources of the Association for Supervision and Curriculum Development (ASCD) and Merrill Education. At www.EducatorLearningCenter.com you will find resources that will enhance your students' understanding of course topics and of current educational issues, in addition to being invaluable for further research.

How will Educator Learning Center help your students become better teachers?

- 600+ articles from the ASCD journal *Educational Leadership* discuss everyday issues faced by practicing teachers.
- Hundreds of lesson plans and teaching strategies are categorized by content area and age range.
- Excerpts from Merrill Education texts give your students insight on important topics of instructional methods, diverse populations, assessment, classroom management, technology, and refining practice.
- Case studies, classroom video, electronic tools, and computer simulations keep your students abreast of today's classrooms and current technologies.
- A direct link on the site to Research Navigator™, where your students will have access to many of the leading education journals as well as extensive content detailing the research process.

What's the cost?

A four-month subscription to Educator Learning Center is $25 but is **FREE** when used in conjunction with this text. To obtain free passcodes for your students, simply contact your local Merrill/Prentice Hall sales representative, and your representative will give you a special ISBN to give your bookstore when ordering your textbooks. To preview the value of this website to you and your students, please go to www.EducatorLearningCenter.com and click on "Demo."

Brief Contents

PART ONE
Theory of Active Experiences 1

1 Experiences and Education: Putting Dewey's Theory Into Practice 3

2 Active Children—Active Environments 13

3 Building Connections to Home and Community Through Active Experiences 29

4 Experiences and Mathematical Content 39

PART TWO
Guides to Active Experiences 49

1 Young Children Develop Ideas of Number and Counting 51

2 Young Children Learn the Basic Concepts of Algebra 69

3 Young Children Learn the Basic Concepts of Geometry 85

4 Young Children Learn the Basic Concepts of Measurement 99

5 Data Description, Organization, Representation, and Analysis 115

6 Math Problem Solving 127

References 139
Resources 143
Index 147

Contents

PART ONE
Theory of Active Experiences 1
---

1 Experiences and Education: Putting Dewey's Theory Into Practice 3

Deep Personal Meaning 4
   Firsthand Experiences 5
   Initiative, Choices, and Decision Making 5
   Age Appropriateness 6
Content with Integrity and Meaning 7
Involving Others 7
   Play 7
   Group Work and Projects 8
   Interactions with Teachers and Other Adults 9
Covered with Language 9
Continuity of Learning 9
Time to Reflect 10
   Organization 11
   Evaluation 11
Summary 12

2 Active Children—Active Environments 13

The Essentials: Health, Safety, Inclusion, and Beauty 15
   Health and Safety 15
   Planning for Inclusion 15
   Beauty 17
Indoor Spaces 18
   Integrating Spaces 18
   Math or Manipulative Areas 18
   Science Areas 19
   Art Centers 19
   Woodworking Centers 20
   Book and Library Centers 20
   Sociodramatic Play Areas 21
   Block Areas 21
   Water and Sand Areas 22

Music Areas 22
Computer Stations 22
Quiet Spaces 23
Outdoor Spaces 23
Math/Science and Nature Discovery Areas 23
Art Spaces 24
Math Spaces 24
Physical Spaces 24
Other Spaces 25
The Teacher's Role 25
Summary 27

3 Building Connections to Home and Community Through Active Experiences 29

Out into the School 31
Inside the School Building 31
Outside in the Natural Environment 31
Out into the Neighborhood and Community 32
Basic Guidelines for Meaningful Field Experiences 32
Building Connections with the Neighborhood and Community 33
The Neighborhood as a Mathematics Laboratory 34
Other Neighborhood Resources 35
The Home-School Connection 36
Summary 38

4 Experiences and Mathematical Content 39

Knowledge of Children 40
Sensorimotor (Birth–2) 40
Preoperational (2–7/8) 41
Knowledge of Subject Matter—Mathematics 42
The Standards 43
Bringing Knowledge of Children and Mathematics Together 44
Expanding and Extending Firsthand Experiences 45
Summary 46

PART TWO
Guides to Active Experiences 49

1 Young Children Develop Ideas of Number and Counting 51

For the Teacher 52
What You'll Need to Know 52
Key Concepts 52

Contents   **xiii**

    Goals and Objectives   53
    What You'll Need   53
    The Home-School Connection   54
    Evaluating and Assessing Children's Learning   54
For the Children   55
    Children Will Develop the Disposition to Count and Use Mathematical Concepts in Their Everyday Lives   55
    Children Will Learn the Names of Numerals and to Write Them   58
    Children Will Learn to Count Sequentially   60
    Children Will Have Meaningful Opportunities to Count Using One-to-One Correspondence   61
    Children Will Begin to Use Number Operations in Connection with Their Daily Activities   62
    Reflecting   63
    Extending and Expanding to the Primary Grades   64
    Documenting Children's Learning   64
Tear-Out Sheets   65

2   Young Children Learn the Basic Concepts of Algebra   69

For the Teacher   70
    What You'll Need to Know   70
    Key Concepts   71
    Goals and Objectives   71
    What You'll Need   71
    The Home-School Connection   74
    Evaluating and Assessing Children's Learning   74
For the Children   75
    The Search for Patterns and Relationships   75
    Sorting, Classifying and Ordering Objects by Size, Number, and Other Properties   76
    Addition and Subtraction of Whole Numbers, Using Objects, Pictures, and Symbols   77
    Reflecting   78
    Extending and Expanding to the Primary Grades   78
    Documenting Children's Learning   79
Tear-Out Sheets   80

3   Young Children Learn the Basic Concepts of Geometry   85

For the Teacher   86
    What You'll Need to Know   86
    Key Concepts   86
    Goals and Objectives   86
    What You'll Need   87
    The Home-School Connection   89
    Evaluating and Assessing Children's Learning   89

For the Children   90
> *Doing Geometry*   90
> *Reflecting*   92
> *Extending and Expanding to the Primary Grades*   93
> *Documenting Children's Learning*   94

Tear-Out Sheets   95

4 Young Children Learn the Basic Concepts of Measurement   99

For the Teacher   100
> *What You'll Need to Know*   100
> *Key Concepts*   100
> *Goals and Objectives*   101
> *What You'll Need*   102
> *The Home-School Connection*   103
> *Evaluating and Assessing Children's Learning*   104

For the Children   105
> *Measuring*   105
> *Extending and Expanding to the Primary Grades*   108
> *Documenting Children's Learning*   109

Tear-Out Sheets   110

5 Data Description, Organization, Representation, and Analysis   115

For the Teacher   116
> *What You'll Need to Know*   116
> *Key Concepts*   116
> *Goals and Objectives*   116
> *What You'll Need*   117
> *The Home-School Connection*   117
> *Evaluating and Assessing Children's Learning*   118

For the Children   119
> *Children Will Collect, Organize, and Sort Data*   119
> *Children Will Begin to Label Information and Develop an Understanding of Scale*   120
> *Children Will Organize Data Through Graphs, Tables, Lists, and So On*   121
> *Children Will Gain Meaning from Graphs, Tables, Lists, and So On*   125
> *Reflecting*   126
> *Extending and Expanding to the Primary Grades*   126
> *Documenting Children's Learning*   126

6 Math Problem Solving   127

For the Teacher   128
> *What You'll Need to Know*   128
> *Key Concepts*   128

Contents

    Goals and Objectives   129
    What You'll Need   129
    The Home-School Connection   129
    Evaluating and Assessing Children's Learning   130
For the Children   130
    Project Work   130
    Children Will Gain Skills in Asking Mathematical Questions   131
    Children Will Gain Skills in Predicting Mathematical Outcomes   132
    Children Will Gain Skills in Observing   133
    Children Will Gain Skills in Comparing and Contrasting   134
    Children Will Gain Skills in Reflecting   135
    Children Will Reach Conclusions   136
    Extending and Expanding to the Primary Grades   136
    Documenting Children's Learning   136
Tear-Out Sheets   137

References   139

Resources   143

Index   147

PART ONE

Theory of Active Experiences

Experiences and Education
Putting Dewey's Theory into Practice

Mathematics learning builds on the curiosity and enthusiasm of children and grows naturally from their experiences.

National Council of Teachers of Mathematics, 2001

Active Experiences for Active Children—Mathematics guides teachers of 3- to 5-year-old children in planning and implementing meaningful mathematical learning experiences for children in childcare settings, nursery schools, Head Start, and kindergarten. This book is based on the idea that activities are simply that—isolated one-shot occurrences. They begin and end quickly. They give children something to do but not something to learn.

Experiences continue. They may last a couple of hours or a day, but usually they continue over weeks, even months. Unlike isolated activities that are fleeting, experiences are filled with learning. According to Dewey's philosophy of learning and teaching (1938), experiences foster learning because they

- hold *deep, personal meaning* for children because they are grounded in children's firsthand experiences with their world, are initiated by the children, and are age appropriate.

- have *meaning and integrity* because the content stems from concepts key to mathematics.

- involve children in *group work and interactions with teachers and other adults,* promoting the skills and attitudes children need to not only perpetuate our democratic society, but also continually improve that society.

- are covered with *language.*

- have *continuity;* one mathematical experience builds on another, forming a complete, coherent, whole, integrated curriculum for young children. Mathematics learning is integrated with literacy, art, science, and even outdoor play. Experiences also continue into children's homes and communities, connecting the curriculum and the early childhood setting to both.

- provide time and the opportunity for children to *reflect* and think about their mathematical experiences so learning occurs.

DEEP PERSONAL MEANING

"High quality mathematics education for three- to six-year old children should . . . enhance children's natural interest in mathematics and their disposition to make sense of their physical and social worlds" (NCTM & NAEYC, 2002, p. 1).

Mathematical experiences enhance children's natural interest because they are meaningful to young children, engaging them in *firsthand* learning in their here-and-now world, encouraging them to *initiate* some of their own learning; are *age-appropriate;* and have meaning and integrity in terms of their *content.*

Firsthand Experiences

"Mathematical learning builds on the curiosity and enthusiasm of children and grows naturally from their experiences" (NCTM, 2001, p. 1). By basing children's learning on mathematical content that can be experienced *firsthand,* a measure of meaning is guaranteed. First, children are not asked to gain knowledge secondhand, by listening to someone else tell them about numbers or the concepts of more or less. Rather, children are involved in challenging mathematical experiences that require meaningful use of numbers. Children learn math through everyday experiences—sorting (putting toys back where they belong), comparing and contrasting (building with blocks), or talking about the daily routine (patterns).

Basing mathematical learning on their firsthand experiences puts children in charge. Because they are the ones using mathematical concepts in connection with their here-and-now experiences, they are the ones who are receiving mathematical information firsthand, and making sense of it.

Piaget's work fully documented that firsthand experiences are necessary if children are to learn, think, and construct mathematical knowledge (Piaget & Inhelder, 1969). When children actually handle objects and things in their environment, they are gaining knowledge of the physical properties of the world in which they live (NCTM & NAEYC, 2002). As children experiment with a wide variety of objects and materials, they learn that some things are heavy, others light. Some are large or small; others are round, square, or rectangular; and still others are triangular in shape. These are concepts that cannot be taught through direct instruction, but can only be learned through firsthand, direct experiences.

When children are engaged in firsthand experiences, their minds are as active as their bodies. By handling objects, counting things, and observing things in their world, children begin to compare them. They classify and sequence objects and things, relating new information to their existing ideas of how the world works, fitting it into their schemas, or ideas. When information doesn't fit their existing schemas, they change these, or create new ones. As they do so, they are constructing their own knowledge and storing it as concepts, rules, or principles (Piaget & Inhelder, 1969).

Then, too, when children act on their environment, they are thinking and figuring out how to do things. They learn how to balance blocks, how to count the napkins needed for a snack or the number of children who can work on the computers. They measure food for pets, divide paper in half and put it together again in another form. Throughout, they are confirming or changing their ideas about mathematical concepts. These initial, often incomplete and tentative, hypotheses and schemas about mathematics build the foundation on which all subsequent learning is based.

Initiative, Choices, and Decision Making

Young children are naturally curious about the world in which they live (NRC, 1996). Mathematical experiences are designed so children can take the *initiative* and make choices and decisions. Children make choices from a variety of centers of interest. Once they have chosen a center to work in, they make decisions about which materials from the center they will use. They may experiment and try something new, or they may simply decide to repeat an action using the same materials over and over again. Either way, children experience success because they select experiences that match their own interests, needs, and developmental level. In this way, children solve the problem of the match Vygotsky (1986) wrote of. As Sue Bredekamp (1998) said, children are "identifying their own zone of proximal development."

Children are asked to take the initiative throughout the day, not just during center time. Real problems that arise from living together offer children opportunities for powerful mathematical learning (NCTM, 2001). Building with unit blocks, children count the blocks needed to balance a tower. Or they measure and count the ingredients for a cooking project, or weigh and measure materials needed to make a rabbit hutch.

Children are also given the opportunity to experience the consequences of their choices. Teachers do not always protect them from making mistakes or from disappointments when they know the result of children's decision making will be less than positive (Dewey, 1944).

By experiencing the consequences of their choices, children have a chance to reflect, to think about their actions, and to determine which they would change, and how or why a decision was or was not effective. In this way they develop mathematical vocabulary, concepts, and the ability to think for themselves, so necessary if children are to become productive citizens of a democratic world.

Dewey saw another purpose for asking children to take the initiative to make choices and decisions (1944). Dewey wanted teachers to use more "stuff" in schools. He asked teachers to include more raw materials and stuff so children could develop concepts and the ability to think. He believed that raw materials such as wood, clay, paints—without any predetermined end or goal for their use—push children into mathematical learning and thinking.

Given blocks, paper, and paint, children must figure out what to do with the materials, how to use them, and when they have achieved their goals. They are the ones who, when failing to achieve a goal, must decide how to change their actions or plans. When they reach a goal, they are the ones who experience the joy of achievement and the satisfaction that comes from thinking and learning. Learning to take the initiative teaches children not to be dependent on others, but to develop an independence of thought and action (Seefeldt, 1993).

Age Appropriateness

Meaningful experiences are *age appropriate*. This book presents challenging mathematical experiences for 3- to 5-year-old children that, at the same time, are achievable. Children are not asked to repeat math concepts they already know, or to achieve goals or objectives clearly beyond their capabilities, development, and maturation.

Experiences that are appropriate to children's developmental level enable children to experience success with mathematics. Feeling successful, children come to think of themselves as numerical learners, who can and will achieve (Bredekamp & Copple, 1997). Research has demonstrated that children's success or failure during their early years predicts the course of later schooling (Alexander & Entwisle, 1988; NRC, 2000). Research shows that the more developmentally appropriate children's early years of schooling, the greater success they will experience when in the primary grades (Charlesworth, Hart, Burts, & DeWolf, 1993; Marcon, 1992).

Before selecting mathematical learning experiences, ask yourself

- Why is this concept worthwhile for this group of children or this individual child? For instance, why do 3-, 4-, or 5-year-old children need to know about multiplication? How would information about multiplication relate to what children already know? How will they use this information?

- Why does this child or group need to learn about numbers now? It may be important to learn about multiplication, but is this something a child needs to know now?

- How efficient is it to teach multiplication or some other mathematical concept to children of this age? There is no trick to teaching young children to do many things—learn to count by rote or even add and subtract by rote. The question is, however, will children learn to count with one-to-one correspondence with accuracy and efficiency when they are older?

Content with Integrity and Meaning

Experiences have meaning and integrity in terms of mathematical content. For example, what mathematical content are children learning when they are asked to color three pigs pink and four pigs brown on a work sheet? Or to mark things on a work sheet that are big and little?

Activities like these are without meaning. Because they have no meaning to children, and because children have no choice in the activity, they only learn that mathematics is a boring, meaningless activity.

Mathematics that has meaning and integrity revolves around concepts key to mathematics. Children's mathematic learning is enhanced when teachers thoughtfully introduce math concepts, language, and methods. Good teachers have always been concerned about fostering children's concept development (Bruner, 1966). Concepts are the ingredients for thinking. They are like mental filing cabinets in which related facts are connected and organized into an ideal. Without a store of concepts, children are limited to understanding their world by dealing with isolated facts and bits of information.

For example, without a concept of *tree,* humans would have to memorize the name of each and every tree they encounter because they could not conceptualize or categorize trees into a singular idea or concept. With the ability to group things into categories, or to think in terms of concepts, we are freed from focusing on each isolated fact. With concepts, children have knowledge of how facts and pieces of information are related and interrelated. They understand something because they've organized the information into a concept; it has meaning to them (Seefeldt, 1997).

Experts from nearly every subject area have identified concepts key to their discipline. These organized concepts give direction and guidance to planning curriculum for young children. All of the concepts presented in *Active Experiences for Active Children—Mathematics* have been selected because they have been identified as key by the National Council of Teachers of Mathematics, the National Education Goals Panel, or other experts in the field.

INVOLVING OTHERS

Interacting with the physical environment is not the only prerequisite for learning mathematics. Children must also interact with their peers, teachers, and other adults if they are to have true mathematical experiences. Both adults and peers are sources of information for children and serve as sounding boards against which children can test the accuracy of their thinking and knowledge (MSDE, 1992; NCTM, 2002). Adults provide access to books and stories with numbers and patterns, to music with actions and directions, or to games that involve rules and taking turns (NCTM, 2001).

Adults also introduce children to the language and conventions of math. Some of mathematical learning is explicit and is simply told to children. This is social knowledge that children cannot construct for themselves. For example, without an adult telling children that the word for this shape is *triangle,* or the name for this numeral is *five,* children would have no way of gaining this knowledge.

Therefore, all of the experiences in this book involve children in play and group work and projects, and in interactions with teachers and other adults.

Play

Children are given the time and opportunity to *play.* Sociodramatic play, which requires other children, is featured. Props relevant to math are placed in the dramatic play areas and on the play yard to encourage children to reflect on and re-create their experiences. Both Vygotsky (1986) and Piaget (Piaget & Inhelder, 1969) believe this type of play leads to symbolic thought. As children play "as if" they were the mother, baby, father, or teacher and "as if" they were counting the days on a calendar or punching numbers on a block that represents a cell phone, they are thinking abstractly. Not only are they using objects to symbolize something not present, but they convince each other that the block is a cell phone.

Other types of play—play with board games, organized circle games, building with blocks, outdoor play, play with puzzles and other materials and manipulatives, even putting toys and blocks back in their places—are also a part of the mathematics curriculum. Each of these types of play gives children practice in observing, sorting, ordering, discriminating, counting, classifying, and predicting.

Rough-and-tumble physical play is just as critical to developing mathematical concepts and learning. Research points out that children only learn in and out, up and down, and other directional concepts by experiencing themselves climbing in and out, running up and down, or being high or low on the jungle gym (Marzoff & DeLoache, 1994; Piaget & Inhelder, 1969).

Group Work and Projects

Children are assigned to a small group to carry out a specific project. Teachers may ask two or three children to go to measure the play yard to find out where a new piece of equipment should go. Others might work together counting the steps it takes to cross the room.

Another type of small group work is arranged. Children may form some of these groups themselves, selecting one or two friends to join them in constructing a skyscraper or some other task. Other groups may include children from another class or of differing ages.

From time to time the entire group of children will meet together. Listening to stories that involve numbers, acting out number finger plays, singing number songs, making decisions about their classroom, sharing news, or listening to a visitor involves the entire community of children. Even for the youngest of children, these thoughtfully planned group meetings are valuable, not just for learning mathematical concepts, but for building a democratic society.

Total group experiences give children practice in following a common idea, arguing a point, listening to others' viewpoints, and forming their own opinions. More importantly, however, they build a sense of community (Dewey, 1944). By singing together, listening to stories, poems, and rhymes together, and sharing news and information, children feel a oneness with others so critical to becoming a member of a democratic society.

The informal give-and-take that occurs as children play with others, work in small groups, or meet together as a total group is important for several reasons. It is through these naturally occurring interchanges that children are challenged to adjust their egocentric thought, assimilating and accommodating differing points of view. Doing so, they develop new ways of understanding the world in which they live. Then, if children are to get along at all when playing and working together as a group, they must consider the ideas, thinking, and wishes of others (Dyson, 1988; Piaget & Inhelder, 1969). As children argue about where the blocks should be stacked, or how to represent the fire truck they saw on a walking field trip, they are gaining the skills involved in taking the perspective of others. To be able to consider that others have views that may differ from one's own is critical for the perpetuation of democracy. The ability to take the perspective of others is necessary if children are to learn to give up some of their own individuality for the good of the group.

Chapter 1 ◆ Experiences and Education

Interactions with Teachers and Other Adults

Dewey's idea that children's education takes place primarily through the process of sharing experiences includes an active role for the teacher and other adults. Arguing against traditional formal education in which a teacher lectures to passive students, Dewey saw the role of the teacher in experiential learning as more demanding, calling for more intimate, complex interactions with children, rather than less guidance and involvement (Dewey, 1938).

Today, it is recognized that children do not learn in isolation and that adult interaction in children's learning and development is not only valuable, but necessary (Bredekamp & Rosegrant, 1995). If children are to learn mathematics through experiences, then teachers and other adults must carefully structure interactions with children and each individual child that are within what Vygotsky (1986) termed the "zone of proximal development." Bredekamp and Rosegrant (1995) describe the zone of proximal development as "teaching on the edge of children's knowledge," so children are challenged to new and higher levels of thinking and learning and are able to successfully achieve these.

COVERED WITH LANGUAGE

Language and experiences go together. You cannot have one without the other. Experiences demand *listening, speaking, writing,* and *reading.*

Experiences give children something in common to talk about. Probably every child in our country has been to a supermarket. But when children go as a group for a specific purpose, they see the store differently. Because they share the same experience, they have a foundation for communicating with one another. From the common experience of going to a supermarket or some other place in the community or school, themes for sociodramatic play, murals, and other group projects emerge. These in turn give children still more to talk about and listen to.

Written language is necessary. Before taking a trip, children must write or dictate a letter to the store manager about the purpose of their trip. They'll need the address of the store, or perhaps they'll want to dial the phone number to speak to the store manager. They also need to write or dictate a list of questions they'll ask the store manager, as well as a thank-you note after their visit. Following the visit, they can draw, paint, construct, or write about their experiences.

Books are consulted and read. Depending on children's needs, these could include reference books, picture dictionaries, and number picture and story books, both factual and fiction. Books are found not just in the library area, but in the housekeeping area, near the blocks, or in the science as well as the mathematics areas.

CONTINUITY OF LEARNING

Because children's growth is continuous, their early mathematical experiences must also be continuous (Barbour & Seefeldt, 1993). One experience builds on another. A thread of meaning runs through a number of experiences, forming a coherent, whole, *continuous* learning curriculum for young children.

Experiences can stem from every discipline. Those in this book revolve around concepts key to mathematics, but other experiences stem from the fields of the biological and physical sciences, the earth sciences, music, dance, and the visual arts, and from the social studies. Each experience is chosen, however, because it builds on a previous one and leads to new experiences. Experiences are chosen not only because they are connected to other experiences, but also because they will enhance, deepen, and strengthen children's concepts, ideas, and perceptions of content.

Experiences continue over time. They are not one-shot occurrences that begin and end quickly. Nor are they units that begin on Monday and end on Friday. Experiences continue, each expanding and extending on the other. Time is given so children can continue to expand and extend their ideas and work. They know as they leave school each day that when they return the next, there will be something for them to continue doing, learning, and experiencing (Katz, 1998).

Teachers in Reggio Emilia, Italy, understand the need for continuity of experiences. The video *To Make a Portrait of a Lion* (Commune di Reggio Emilia, 1987) illustrates how children's interests in stone lions guarding one of the village squares led to a yearlong study of lions. Children sat on the lions, drew them, looked at pictures of lions in books, visited museums to see other portrayals of lions, and learned where lions live.

When mathematical experiences are continuous, children have the time and opportunity to see relationships between facts, to develop mathematical ideas, to generalize, to extrapolate, and to make a tentative intuitive leap into new knowledge. This leap, from merely learning a number name or fact to connecting one fact to another, is an essential step in the development of mathematical thinking (Bruner, 1966).

Continuity should extend across children's early childhood years. This means curriculum experiences should be coordinated and continuous from one school placement to the next. Thus, *Active Experiences for Active Children—Mathematics* offers suggestions for extending and expanding experiences so they can form a complete whole as children progress from preschool to kindergarten, and into the early primary grades.

Just as experiences serve to integrate the curriculum and connect children's thinking, so can they serve to unite home and school. This book demonstrates how to involve parents in children's math learning. Each experience specifies a role for children's families so families will be active partners with teachers in the education of their children in mathematics.

TIME TO REFLECT

Children are given time and the opportunity to *reflect* and think about their experiences. Dewey (1938) maintained that it is only as children are able to reflect on an experience that they are truly engaged in learning.

Reflection can take a number of forms. Children need the time and opportunity to *pull away* and be by themselves so they can think and reflect on what they are doing. At other times children will be asked to reflect on their experiences by *organizing* their ideas, *presenting* them to others, *applying* their knowledge, *communicating* it to others, and *evaluating* their experiences.

Being able to *pull away* for a while and think and reflect on an experience is necessary. Young children in group care or educational settings especially need space, time, and freedom to be alone once in a while.

In addition to being alone and thinking, pulling away can also mean children will listen to tapes or CDs, view videos, or look at and read books all by themselves. But it is perfectly acceptable to foster reflection by allowing and even encouraging children to daydream, sit and observe others, or play alone in a center.

Organization

Children can *organize* their experiences in different ways. They might create a display to illustrate what they have learned. One kindergarten group studied rocks. With the teacher helping them, children classified different types of rocks they found in their community; counted and graphed rocks, identifying which type of rock was most prevalent; and labeled rocks and placed them on a table. The teacher added photographs of the children finding different rocks, and a title for the display.

Children in the childcare centers of Reggio Emilia are often asked to organize their ideas by making displays that document their experiences and what they have learned. One group organized their knowledge of mazes by constructing a large maze on their play yard, measuring as they went along.

Teachers can help children present their ideas through bar graphs or other types of graphs to organize an experience. A kindergarten class tasted a variety of seeds and voted for their favorite seed. The teacher then made a graph of their votes.

Or an individual or a small group of children might make a *presentation* to the total group. Children could tell about their experiences, perhaps showing how tall the corn grew, or how many seeds actually sprouted.

Children can be asked to *apply* their knowledge. They might use their knowledge of numbers to plan snacks for the group, select a specific number of friends with whom to play a game, or count the days until their birthday.

Dewey believed that an experience is not complete until it has been communicated to another person. That is why children are asked to draw, paint, or write about their experiences, *communicating* their ideas to others.

At times, children might be encouraged to communicate something they've imagined, rather than experienced. Imagination is a form of thinking, and children enjoy drawing or painting an imaginary trip to the moon, illustrating an imaginative story, or creating an imaginary ending to a favorite story.

Evaluation

Finally, children are asked to *evaluate* their mathematical learning. Even 3-year-olds can be asked to think about what they did during the day. Four-year-olds, in addition to thinking about the things they did, can also begin to think about how they have grown and what they have learned. By 5 years of age children can pick out their best math work to include in a portfolio, decide how completely they gained a math or other skill, and rate themselves on how well they accomplished specific tasks. They can also be asked to tell about all the things they know now that they did not know at the beginning of the year, or when they were younger, and to tell what they want to learn next and how they could learn it (Seefeldt & Barbour, 1998).

Teachers take time to reflect on their work and children's learning as well. Daily they reflect on their program and the mathematics curriculum, asking themselves

- How far have I come in achieving my goals for myself and the children?
- What routines, interactions with the children, and experiences will I repeat tomorrow?
- Which things will I change?

And they find ways to evaluate children's learning. They observe children informally as they work and play together, talk with them individually to find out what each child understands about mathematics and what will challenge each, collect samples of work to include in portfolios, and use checklists to determine how children are progressing.

SUMMARY

Children learn mathematics from experiences because they are involved hands-on, minds-on, and actively engaged in making sense of themselves in their world. Because mathematical experiences are embedded in children's here-and-now world, they are of interest to children. This interest motivates children to meet the challenges of the experience and become successful math learners.

Mathematics experiences continue. When children leave school for the day, they should always know there will be something for them to continue doing when they return the next day. The fact that experiences are based on concepts key to mathematics not only gives them intellectual integrity, but offers children continuity of content. And because experiences are connected to children's homes and communities, there is a continuous thread of learning in children's lives.

By using language, working with others, and having the opportunity to think and reflect on their mathematical experiences, children are active participants in their classroom community. This participation prepares them to take their place as knowledgeable, active citizens of a democratic society.

2

Active Children—Active Environments

Curricula have been published that apply mathematical problem solving to real-world problems; teachers are using theme centers such as the "grocery store" or the "ice cream shop" that use manipulatives and props to enhance the application of mathematical concepts . . .

Basile, 1999, p. 156

Centers of learning are ideally suited for the development of emergent mathematics thinking in young children. Through multiple theme centers, children have the opportunity to explore, develop, discuss, test, and apply mathematical ideas in a variety of contexts. They are also ideally suited for the social interaction essential to the child's construction of meaning in math as in all subject matter areas. Rich and challenging classroom talk between children and adult-child dialogue foster peer-based learning and assistance from more competent adults to reach higher conceptual levels.

The range of skills that can be achieved with adult guidance and peer collaboration far exceeds what a child can learn alone or in whole class instruction. According to Greenes (1999), the teacher must not only model the investigative process for the children, formulating conjectures and asking questions, but also help the children to make connections among important mathematical ideas. This chapter presents general guidelines for designing environments for children—health and safety, inclusion, and beauty. More emphasis in placed on mathematics centers, but the whole environment is considered as a laboratory for learning math.

If active children are to learn through active experiences, then their environment must be carefully, thoughtfully, and deliberately arranged. Spaces should be structured so children can

- engage in meaningful firsthand learning, taking the initiative for their learning and making choices and decisions;

- work, play, and interact freely with others, both peers and adults;

- use language, talking, listening, writing, and reading in connection with their interactions;

- experience success as they gain new skills through interaction with their physical environment;

- be actively introduced to mathematical concepts, methods, and language through a range of teaching strategies; and

- be alone and in groups to reflect on their experiences.

Beginning with the essentials—health, safety, inclusion, and beauty—teachers plan for children's meaningful learning experiences by deliberately arranging the indoor and outdoor learning environments. Teachers not only deliberately arrange physical environments for active learning, but they also plan ways of interacting with children that foster and promote children's learning and development.

THE ESSENTIALS: HEALTH, SAFETY, INCLUSION, AND BEAUTY

Health and Safety

Specific health and safety concerns are delineated for each of the activities suggested in the experience chapters to come. The following are more general concerns for the indoor and out-of-doors environment:

- Equipment is checked for sharp edges, splinters, loose pieces that could cause accidents, and small parts that children might swallow or stuff in their ears.
- Most materials provided for the children are unbreakable, although in some instances, such as making an aquarium, glass is the best choice, and adult guidance is essential.
- Equipment is disinfected by daily washing with detergent in water, rinsing with clear water, wiping or spraying with a solution of two tablespoons of chlorine bleach and one gallon of water, and sun or air drying.
- Use of all heat sources is well supervised, and outlets are covered when not in use.
- Tubs and pools of water are closely supervised.
- Tools such as knives and hammers are in good condition, and their use is carefully observed.
- Parents are contacted about any allergies that would prevent their child from participating in a particular math-based activity such as cooking.

Safety is a fundamental concern. Teachers must know and apply the necessary safety regulations in the storage, use, and care of the materials used by students. Locked cabinets are a must when some materials are not in use. In addition, careful rules must be established for the care of fish and small animals if they reside in the classroom. There are many mathematics concepts to be gained from the care and feeding of small animals: "How much do we feed the gerbil in the morning?" "How high do we fill the container?" "How much has the gerbil grown?" "How much does the gerbil weigh?" "Which one is the largest?"

Teachers need to examine their feelings about having pets reside in the classroom. Too often, classroom pets live under poor conditions. Children have not been instructed in the proper handling of them, nor is there a place for them to go on weekends and holidays. Many children have allergies to various types of animals. If pets are to be a part of the math learning environment, children should observe them and communicate about them each day. See *Active Experiences for Active Children—Science* (Seefeldt & Galper, 2002) for more discussion of classroom animals.

Some teachers operate under the mistaken assumption that they are free from any responsibility for children's learning when the class is outside. These teachers see outdoor play as a break for themselves and an opportunity to talk with other adults. This attitude fosters aggressive and unsafe play. Some general safety and health considerations for active outdoor environments are described on page 16.

Additionally, play yards are accessible to children with disabilities, foster their independence, and enhance skill development. See the following section.

Planning for Inclusion

The physical environment can be arranged in ways that enable all children to participate to the fullest extent possible in all experiences. According to Flynn and Kieff (2002), adaptations may be applicable to inside environments, but are *critical* for the outside.

> **GENERAL SAFETY AND HEALTH CONSIDERATIONS FOR ACTIVE OUTDOOR ENVIRONMENTS**
>
> - Fencing at least 4 feet high surrounds the play yard.
> - All surfaces are properly maintained and checked for debris such as broken glass and animal waste.
> - All plantings within the fence are nonpoisonous.
> - Outdoor play equipment is inspected daily for missing or broken parts, splinters, and sharp edges.
> - Sandboxes have a retractable cover.
> - Play area is well drained—water is not allowed to stand.
> - Soil is tested for lead and other toxic substances.
> - Fresh soil is brought in for digging and for gardens when necessary.
> - Climbing and sliding equipment is anchored firmly in soft ground cover at least 1 foot deep.
> - Equipment is developmentally appropriate (or can be adapted) for the age/stage of the children using it.
> - Railings enclose high equipment to protect from falls.
> - Equipment is spaced for safe movement between pieces.

To permit the use of a wheelchair, remove physical barriers, provide wider paths, and arrange work spaces and activity units to offer shelter from intrusion or interference (Louglin & Suina, 1982). More accomplished peers may model and teach the use of mathematics tools both inside and outside the classroom. When safety is an issue, a "buddy" may be assigned to a child who is less able. Children with special needs (as well as those without) may profit from a multisensory approach to the teaching of mathematics.

Reducing the amount of visual stimulation in a given area aids children who are visually impaired. Teachers have found that they can add textures or raised patterns to the walls to enable visually impaired children to locate themselves in space. On the playground, children should be oriented to the major playground features that can be used as points of reference. Tactile experiences are also valuable for nonimpaired peers since they foster learning through touch. Others find small shelving units, with a few materials on each shelf, also helpful for children who become overstimulated easily.

Hearing-impaired children require more visual stimulation and less auditory distraction. Felt pads on tabletops, carpeted shelves and other work surfaces, as well as the clear display of all materials and equipment will assist the child (Seefeldt & Barbour, 1998). Flynn and Kieff (2002) suggest the provision of outdoor toys and materials that use the other senses available to the child, including touch, smell, and movement. Teachers may actively foster children's understanding and appreciation of the senses and sensory impairments through active experiences with the five senses. For a chapter on the senses of the human body, see *Active Experiences for Active Children—Science* (Seefeldt & Galper, 2002).

Mallory (1998) suggests that small groups of two to four learners provide an optimal structure for fostering cognitive development and social participation in inclusive classrooms: "Given the heterogeneity that exists in inclusive classrooms, it is logical to assume that whole group activity is not likely to be an effective means for assuring that the particular needs of individual learners will be met" (p. 228). For a good discussion of specific outdoor adaptations to meet the individual needs of children with blindness or low vision, deafness or hearing loss, physical challenges, autism spectrum disorder, and cognitive delays, see the article "Including Everyone in Outdoor Play" in *Young Children 57 (3), 20–26*, by L. L. Flynn and J. Kieff (2002).

Beauty

Aesthetics and beauty must be considered for young children growing up in a world that increasingly prefers highways and large housing developments to green space and historic buildings. Aesthetics means being sensitive to beauty in the environment—in nature and art. "Such sensitivity is fostered not by talking about beauty but by experiencing it in a variety of forms" (Wilson, 1995, p. 4). It is important to note that beauty resides not only in the natural environment, but also in vibrant city neighborhoods, small historic towns, and school classrooms around the world.

The childcare centers in Reggio Emilia, Italy, illustrate the wonder and beauty of environments created with aesthetics in mind. Stepping into a childcare center in Reggio, one knows immediately that the environment has been carefully arranged to simplify and order the children's world as well as surround them with beauty (Seefeldt, 1995).

Open rooms, filled with light and air, are simply and elegantly arranged. This clear, clean conceptualization of an environment is especially appropriate for active children who learn through active experiences, and facilitates the child's construction of beginning mathematics concepts. Integrating conceptual learning in various subject matter areas with artistic expression, children are encouraged to make visual or symbolic representations of their activities using a variety of media and techniques. For example, the children's re-creation of various patterns found in nature facilitates math learning.

Everywhere you look there is something beautiful to wonder over and ponder. Mirrors of all types are found throughout the center. Bits of mirrors and colored glass hang in front of windows to catch a sunbeam and bounce it back to children. Long horizontal mirrors are mounted near the floor so children can watch themselves as they build with blocks or play with others.

Plants and flowers are present throughout the center in classrooms, in lunchrooms and sleeping rooms, and in the bathrooms. Children's artwork is mounted, framed, and displayed, serving not only to stimulate children to thought and permit them to document and reflect on past experiences, but also to inform others of the experiences children are having in and out of the center. As in good practice in the United States, the home is intimately connected with the centers.

This emphasis on aesthetics in Reggio "reflects an appreciation of detail and sensitivity to design consistent with the Italian cultural tradition of creative endeavors" (Mallory & New, 1994, p. 10). Nevertheless, children everywhere, not just in Italy, deserve to live and learn in environments that are aesthetically pleasing and visually appealing (Seefeldt & Barbour, 1998). Bredekamp (1993) reflects "that perhaps we, in America, have set our sights too low in our vision of excellence" (p.13). Too often in programs for young children, little attention is given to the beauty of the classroom and outdoor space. Commercial posters and decorations take the place of objects of beauty and child-inspired art. Then, too, the connections between the world of art and the world of mathematics are ignored. As children create works of art they learn about the use of space, line, direction, two- and three-dimensional shapes, patterns, relative measurement, geometry, and many more basic mathematics concepts.

INDOOR SPACES

Integrating Spaces

Organizing indoor spaces with centers of interest permits active children to engage in active experiences. Centers of interest are those areas of the room that are clearly defined with either actual dividers or suggested boundaries. They contain materials and equipment organized to promote specific types of learning. The materials are carefully arranged so children can see the choices available and make decisions about which materials they will use and how they will use them (Bronson, 1995). Schools participating in the Boston University–Chelsea Project for mathematics learning organized their classrooms around multiple theme centers—for block construction, water exploration, art, reading, computers, gardens, a store, and a kitchen. Children moved among the centers, generally in groups of two to five (Greenes, 1999).

Yet, while areas are defined, teachers will want to work toward an integrated curriculum framework so that mathematics, for example, becomes a part of the social studies, arts and crafts, music and movement, and emergent literacy (for younger children) or the language arts (for older children). Math and science form a natural alliance, and many curriculum materials are designed to integrate the two. For excellent suggestions on play materials for the classroom, see *The Right Stuff for Children Birth to 8: Selecting Play Materials to Support Development* (Bronson, 1995).

Children's literature, for example, is an excellent way to integrate mathematics throughout the early childhood curriculum. An important part of an effective math curriculum is a classroom library with a wide variety of math-related children's literature, both fiction and nonfiction. The experience chapters that follow have extensive children's literature suggestions for teaching each mathematics concept area identified by the National Association for Teaching Mathematics for the early childhood years.

Math or Manipulative Areas

While opportunities for learning emergent mathematics concepts abound in all classroom centers, children are continually drawn to an area of the room that offers them a variety of play materials that may be manipulated and explored to foster math learning. Materials should be kept to a reasonable quantity so that children do not become distracted and frustrated. New materials may be introduced as children master or become tired of the old ones. Following are some possibilities for play materials that foster math concepts:

- Cardboard, wood, and plastic puzzles. The number of pieces and the complexity will vary with the age of the child. Clock and number puzzles directly relate to math learning, as do simple puzzles with shapes divided into fractions.
- Beads and string to foster pattern-making and the copying of sequential patterns.
- Other pattern-making materials such as small blocks and tiles, mosaic blocks, color cubes, magnetic form boards, pegboards, plastic shapes, paper shapes and strips, and block printing equipment.
- Materials for matching, sorting, ordering, and comparing (by shape, size, texture, number, color, or concept).
- Objects to count, order, and match to numbers.
- Games such as concentration (matching), lotto, dominoes, and counting. Older children may enjoy bingo.
- A few decks of regular cards.

- Coins to sort and count. Young children should be introduced to money although they are not yet ready to use it correctly. For example, many still think that the larger the coin the more it is worth.

Construction sets, Tinkertoys, Erector sets, and large Legos may find a home here or with the blocks, depending on the intent of the children's activity. The teacher will want to provide materials that will excite a child's natural interest, pose many questions, and promote active inquiry. Whatever active experiences spring from the children's interests or the teacher's plans, it is important that enough time is available for children to reflect upon their learnings and, if they wish, to maintain their work in progress and to display their results. Teachers will want to pose questions to the children so that they may begin to build their mathematics vocabulary. Beginning to build mathematics understanding in children takes time on a daily basis and over the school year.

Science Areas

As mentioned previously, math and science are natural allies. When children learn science, they are often also learning about math as well. The science center should provide opportunities for children to observe, classify, compare, measure, communicate, experiment, make predictions, and reach conclusions.

One teacher arranged a pitcher of water and some small cups on a table next to small containers of instant coffee, tea leaves, dirt, sand, beans, sugar, and salt. She posed a question for the children: "Which things will dissolve in water and which ones will not?" A clipboard with a checklist for children to record their findings was placed beside the center. Children were encouraged to discuss and negotiate their conclusions.

Other science learning centers could be equipped with scales of all types, measurement tools, and things to weigh, measure, and balance. The teacher would pose questions such as "Which one is heavier?" "Which is longer?" and so on. Children can record their conclusions in journals or on checksheets created by the teacher.

Machines to take apart—clocks, pencil sharpeners, instrument-panel boards (all of which have been safety proofed)—along with screwdrivers and wrenches fascinate children, who are curious about how things work. One group of 5-year-olds worked for days taking apart an alarm clock and recorded each step in detailed drawings that the teacher displayed to document the process and then stored for later reflection.

Art Centers

Through the visual arts, children are able to give expression to their ideas, imaginations, feelings, and emotions. This expression is necessary if children are to reflect on their experiences. Each day, children should have a choice of whether to draw, paint, model, cut and paste, or construct something. Materials are arranged on tables or shelves that are easily accessible to children. Easels, a variety of brushes, and fresh, thick paints are available every day. At other times, areas of the floor, or a table or two, can also be used for painting. All types of drawing materials—crayons, markers, chalk, even pencils for older children—are stored in open shelves for children's selection (Dighe, Calomiris, & Van Zutphen, 1998). A junk box, with every type of material imaginable, and a sewing box for 5-year-olds, equipped with threads, bits of fabric, buttons, and large blunt needles, are available. There is a separate area for clay and modeling materials.

Because the visual arts give children a way to organize, reflect upon, and present their ideas or emotions, art materials are chosen that enable children to do so. For example, a group of children went to the Folk Museum to see an exhibit on quilts. When they returned, they found the art center equipped with a variety of papers and cloth in various shapes, scissors, glue, and were given the opportunity to make their own or a shared quilt from the shapes.

Manipulating modeling clay and observing its properties, painting with tempera paints and observing drips and how colors mix, and organizing and sorting materials for a collage help children to understand math concepts and integrate them with other subject matter areas.

Woodworking Centers

Woodworking involves such a variety of skills, tools, and materials that there are endless opportunities for using the processes of mathematics such as classification, comparison, understanding spatial relationships, measurement, and the visualization of things in three-dimensional form. Through trial and error and careful use of questions by the teacher, children will also draw conclusions such as "That nail is larger" or "The small nail will work better." Children are endlessly fascinated by woodworking, but teachers must closely supervise and co-construct learnings with their students.

A place for children to construct three-dimensional objects should also be included. Children can work with any material. In Reggio Emilia, found objects—boxes, feathers, shells, sequins, paper, silk and brocade scraps—are stored (and classified) on open shelves in aesthetically pleasing ways, inviting children to choose what materials they will use and how they will arrange them. The design and creation of three-dimensional objects help children to master math concepts.

Book and Library Centers

The library area is a place where books are arranged along with tables, chairs, soft carpet, and cushions enticing children to stay and read. It is a place located away from other distractions where children will find every type of book—poetry, fiction, folktales, picture books, informational books and materials, biography, and books composed of photographs. Math can be found in all of these genres of children's literature. The authors have highlighted the children's books appropriate for learning in each concept area. (See experience chapters.)

All children should find themselves reflected in these books. Books depicting the lives of children with special needs, as well as children of diverse cultural, racial, and ethnic backgrounds, will be selected (Blaska & Lynch, 1998). This is especially important in the area of mathematics. "In mathematics as in literacy, children who live in poverty and who are members of linguistic and ethnic minority groups demonstrate significantly lower levels of achievement" (NAEYC & NCTM, 2002, p. 1).

Catalogues, sections from the newspaper specifically geared to children's work, and children's newspapers and magazines are fun to include. Children can use catalogues as "wish books" or can compare, contrast, or classify the contents. Mounted pictures cut from magazines and depicting a topic the children are studying are excellent for younger children to sort through and carry around with them. Books dictated or written by the children are favorites. Some library areas also include flannel boards with cut-out figures for children to put into sequence or to use to retell a story by themselves or with a group of children.

Some books may be organized as a take-home library for the children so their learning experiences can continue when they are at home. Linking mathematics with literature is a natural way for parents to extend and support math in the home. A simple checkout sheet with two markers attached can be mounted above the books. The children can place a check with the red marker when they take out a book and a check with the black marker when they return it. Books will also be displayed around the room. In one Head Start center, children went for a tour of the local food store. When they returned to their classroom, they found several books on how to set up a store, going to the store with parents, specialty stores, and large supermarkets. Children began consulting these as they created a small market with boxes, scales, and models of fruit and vegetables all classified into sections of the center. They also became concerned with money and how to determine the cost of each product.

Although both nonfiction and fiction books can be used to support the development of math concepts, it is important that the information is accurate. The books should further spur children to investigate something or engage in hands-on math experiences.

Sociodramatic Play Areas

The primary sociodramatic play area is the housekeeping center, where children engage in playing house with others, enacting the roles they observe in their homes. Other organizational schemes are also possible, as reflected in the Boston University–Chelsea Projects for Mathematics Learning, where a kitchen and store were permanent centers.

Props reflecting children's home life are found in the housekeeping area. Some may reflect their parents' work world—briefcases, hard hats, work boots, or tools representative of parents' work. Other items such as dishes, pots and pans, baby dolls representing all ethnic groups, cribs, baby bottles, full-length and hand mirrors, alarm clocks, microwaves, discarded cell phones, calculators, computers, and clothes of all types will reflect children's life at home.

Based on children's experiences with their world, other dramatic play areas will be pertinent. Notice how teachers can build emergent math concepts into each. For instance, if children have visited

- a post office, then a post office with envelopes, stamps, machines to weigh objects, and cubbyholes in which to sort mail would be created.

- a fast-food restaurant, then a restaurant with aprons, hats, trays, boxes for food, cups and bottles, a cash register, and pretend money would be added.

- a supermarket, then a store, complete with a cash register, money, all types of food containers, cans, boxes, bags to pack items, old cash register receipts, and other materials, would be arranged so children could reenact their visit to the supermarket, taking turns being shoppers, clerks, bakers, or shelf stockers. Each of these roles involves the use of math. As "store play" continues, the play will be expanded to include more and more math concepts.

Block Areas

Blocks and spaces in which to build are essential to a math curriculum. As children build with blocks, they indulge in activities that begin to fulfill the standards for instructional programs proposed by the NCTM (2000). Block building involves numbers and operations, patterns and functions, geometry, measurement, and data analysis. Bronson (1995) suggests

- wooden unit blocks (80–100 pieces per child playing), including specialized forms (arches, curves)

- large hollow blocks

- plastic bricks

- for children age 4 and older, various types of interlocking blocks, except metal or those smaller than one-half inch

- outdoor building materials

Ideally, indoor blocks should be stored on open shelves with a place for each type of block. Storing all rectangular blocks on the same shelf, for example, fosters children's ability to classify. A complete set of wooden unit blocks is the best investment a center or program can make. If these are unaffordable, blocks can be made out of paper cartons. Math concepts are fostered as children observe, build, measure, compare, estimate or predict, begin to learn about spatial relations, and construct building plans.

Water and Sand Areas

Children need indoor areas where they can explore the properties of both water and sand. Water is easy to provide. All that is needed is a low table; a small, plastic pan; some plastic containers—cups, spoons, funnels, plastic tubing, straws; and a small amount of water. Preschool children learn about volume as they pour sand or water from one container to another. They also experiment with filling larger containers with the contents of smaller ones, and make estimates about how much it will take to fill a given container.

Sand, in a sand table, a plastic tub, or an old wading pool, can readily be available indoors. As with water play, children learn beginning math concepts through the use of a variety of containers from which to pour and measure sand, or mold and shape sand into various forms. Water should be handy if children are to build with sand. Young children are often observed creating environments such as castles and cities in the sand table. This fosters concepts of placement in space and early mapping skills. Small objects can be added to the sand table to expand children's concept of space and location.

Music Areas

The music area should be a space in which to listen to, as well as make, music. Here, children listen to a tape, operate a CD player by themselves, or play whatever musical instruments the center can provide. Kim (1999) suggests that many musical experiences are closely related to mathematical knowledge. For example, "slow and fast" is a concept that young children can easily understand and that the teacher can relate to classification and comparison. Too, young children can explore a variety of patterns through musical activities such as introducing strong and weak beats and long and short sounds. Similarly, verbal counting can be improved through vocalizing rhymes and songs.

Computer Stations

Several computers can be set up with age-appropriate programs that

- teach some skills more effectively than traditional and less expensive methods and materials.
- have the potential to help children develop higher-order thought skills like judging, evaluating, analyzing, and synthesizing information (Wright & Shade, 1994).
- present accurate information.
- provide for more than one child to work with a program.
- teach a concept or concepts that children are unable to obtain through an active experience or inquiry.

Clements (1999) believes that a vision for the use of computers de-emphasizes rote practice on isolated facts and emphasizes discussing and solving problems in geometry, number sense, and patterns with the help of manipulatives and computer software.

Quiet Spaces

Children need space to be alone or to interact with one or two others. It may be a corner of the room with a few pillows on the floor, a small nook in the library area, or a chair and table somewhere away from other centers. Every classroom needs a space—wherever it is, or whatever it consists of—where children can be away from the group, relax, calm themselves, and think.

OUTDOOR SPACES

The out-of-doors is really an extension of the stimulating, well-arranged indoor learning environment. The added richness of natural surroundings and open spaces enhances possibilities for active math learning experiences. Teachers will want to expand water and sand play out-of-doors. Digging in the dirt and extracting different sizes of pebbles and rocks provides information to a child about the nature of the surfaces of the earth and the concepts of heavy and light, rough and smooth, and large and small. Learnings are best reinforced when teachers use questions to focus children on their inquiries. For example, when examining rocks, focusing questions might be "Which ones would you put in the pile of smooth ones?" or "Can you make a pile of rough ones?"

Math activities occur in special spaces arranged for the young child's emergent concept development. They are also intimately connected and integrated with all areas of the early childhood curriculum.

Math/Science and Nature Discovery Areas

Spaces should be designated for exploration and discovery. These include the following:

- An area set aside for bird feeders, birdhouses, and birdbaths. Children can observe and record from a distance the comings and goings of a variety of birds, their nests, and the foods they eat. This provides an excellent opportunity for data collection and analysis.

- An outside sandbox. While an indoor sand table provides children with many active experiences with science, an outside sandbox has many advantages. Children can climb into it, sit in the sand while playing in it, and create on a large scale. The sand area should be adjacent to a water source. To expand the possibilities for math concept learning, props should be added such as containers of all sizes, cooking utensils, measurement tools, and sand molds.

- A carefully supervised wading pool or water table. Water play gives children essential skills in pouring, measuring, and comparing volume. Outside, much more splashing and spilling is acceptable, and water can be carried around the play yard. Many items may be added as required by the type of investigation children are pursuing. For example, young children can explore the capacity of various containers by direct comparisons or by counting the number of cups required to fill each one.

- A garden area for various types of plants, flowers, and vegetables. This space should be carefully placed beyond the limits of children's active play and close to a water source so that very young children can be involved in nurturing the plantings. Some teachers may want to reserve part of the gardening area for impromptu digging where children learn about the composition of soil, the insects and worms that make their homes there, and the organic matter that decomposes to produce soil. The area should be arranged to receive at least six hours of sunlight a day. In locations where this is not possible, teachers and children together should plan gardens that flourish in the shade. The garden area provides a wealth of mathematics experiences: counting, finding patterns, measuring the growth of plants, comparing the growth of two or more plants, and deciding how much water flowers and vegetables need.

These suggestions are for a planned approach to using the school yard as a math (and science) discovery center. They may be supplemented by carefully chosen trips.

Art Spaces

Just about any art activity can take place outside. From painting with water on school walls or sheds to painting with color on large brown paper strips hanging on a playground fence, children and teachers can enjoy aesthetic experiences with the knowledge that cleanup will be simple. Through exploring shapes and patterns that can be drawn or constructed on a larger scale in the out-of-doors, children build math concepts. Children can draw on the hard surfaces with large pieces of chalk of various colors dipped in water. Teachers can encourage them to try patterns by repeating the colors in a predictable order. Their creations will wash away with the next rain. Or they can use crayons or markers on large papers spread on a hard surface or on tables.

Modeling with clay and other materials is fun to do outside, as is building with boxes, found objects, and other materials. Through their constructions, children learn about the attributes of things, and discover which are effective and ineffective in creating satisfactory structures. Measurement and number, as well as the ability to estimate, are involved in creating structures that work, and when things fall apart, children can make inferences about suitable and unsuitable choices.

Math Spaces

The out-of-doors helps children to understand direction, distance, and position in space through group games and individual explorations. Math skills are intimately intertwined with those required for grasping science concepts. Outside, it is possible to use numbers to count things, and place them in order. Children may estimate quantities of rocks or trees by using their observational skills. The smooth stones one child gathers, the acorns another collects, the sticks or plastic cups in the sandbox, the number of children waiting to ride a new trike—all these give children something concrete to count. Children also classify the stones, insects, seeds, and acorns they find, or place them in order from smallest to largest, heaviest to lightest. Shapes such as circles, squares, and triangles can be used to describe many things that can be seen in the play yard, in the natural environment, or in buildings viewed from the outside.

Children learn about math and the physical world through materials, small pieces of equipment, and props that can be moved around and with which they can build and be creative. With movable equipment, children can construct their own play environments using boxes, boards, barrels, tires, and tubes.

Physical Spaces

Space and a variety of stationary and movable equipment foster running, jumping, and climbing out-of-doors. Equipment that promotes social interactions, use of language, and cooperative play, and is rich with potential for children to form concepts of the physical properties of their world includes the following:

- Large wooden crates and boxes, boards with cleats, and large hollow blocks.
- Climbing equipment that comes in several movable sections—such as a trestle unit, a climbing gate, or an A-frame unit—that can be arranged and rearranged to meet children's changing interests or needs. Playhouses often come designed with storage sheds below.
- Cable tables of assorted sizes, tree trunks with sharp branches removed, and sturdy wooden barrels.
- Balance beams, an old log, several logs placed end to end, a board placed on its side, or stepping stones, patio stones, or old tires placed in a series give children a sense of different ways to handle their bodies in space.
- A wide assortment of balls of all sizes and weights.
- Things to push, pull, and ride.

Other Spaces

Ideally, outdoor environments should include sections with different surfaces such as grass, concrete, earth, and sand. Pine bark, cedar chips, or pine needles can be used to create soft areas, while other surfaces can be paved for playing organized games, which give children a sense of using their bodies in space. Play yards should have a balance of sun and shade, active areas for large motor activities, and quiet areas where a child might take a book, listen to music, or play with small manipulatives. Attention should be given to different terrains. A balance of levels can make the play yard visually interesting and provide hills for climbing and rolling down as well as flat surfaces. Outdoor pathways may be created to wind around the outside play environment to define various interest areas. They can be created of cedar chips, stones, or cement.

When discussing math concept formation, NCTM (2000) highlights the importance of tools. Teachers will want to add tools of all types such as thermometers, rulers, tape measures, scales, and containers of all sizes and shapes to aid children in their observations and explorations. Simple cameras provide an excellent way for young children to document discoveries in the outdoor environment.

THE TEACHER'S ROLE

> Teachers need to know and use "mathematics for teaching" that combines mathematical knowledge and pedagogical knowledge. They must be information providers, planners, consultants, and explorers of uncharted mathematical territory. (NCTM, 2000, p. 370)

Without a concerned, interested, and knowledgeable adult, even the best equipped and planned spaces fall short of offering children meaningful experiences. Based on knowledge of children and, of their experiences at home and in the community, it is the adult who

- selects, arranges, and changes indoor and outdoor centers, making sure the spaces remain safe, inviting, and accessible to all children.
- schedules large blocks of time during the morning and afternoon for active experiences. Mathematics is built into all areas of the curriculum, but it cannot be left to chance; time is scheduled to focus in on a particular mathematics concept.
- provides a background of meaningful experiences with people, places, and things so children will have ideas to express through play.

Most of all, however, it is the teacher who interacts with children in ways that clarify, extend, and expand their knowledge and skills.

- Teachers observe and supervise children as they play. Observations can focus on the total group of children or on individuals. (See tear-out assessment instruments at the end of the experience chapters.) The progress children are making, the skills they are gaining, and the things they still need to learn can be noted. When needed, the teacher steps in to support children in their attempts to learn new concepts, skills, and attitudes.
- Teachers enter into joint activities with children, working collaboratively with them on a problem or task, such as comparing seeds from four different familiar plants.
- Teachers use language to promote children's learning, naming things in the children's environment and giving information when needed. Discourse builds students' conceptual knowledge and gives teachers valuable information for assessing progress and planning next steps.
- Teachers ask a variety of questions that help children to expand concepts and to build vocabulary: "Let's count how many children are wearing red today; how many did you count?" "Is your suitcase light or heavy?" "Can you find something in the room that is about as long as your foot?"
- Teachers offer assistance to help a child solve a problem or achieve the next level of functioning: "Here, I'll hold the tape measure for you while you pull it to the end of the table."
- Teachers plan and help children select activities that are appropriate for individual children's development and background of experiences. "If instructional materials are not consistent with the expectations of families and community members or do not seem reasonable to them, serious difficulties can arise" (NCTM, 2000, p. 369). The selection and implementation of curricular materials must be a collaborative process.
- Teachers serve as models, displaying the attitudes and skills they want for the children. They demonstrate how to do something, supporting children as they try.
- When needed, teachers give specific directions and information.
- Teachers set expectations for classroom behaviors that are consistent with children's emerging cognitive and social capabilities (Berk and Winsler, 1995).
- Teachers seriously enter into conversations about children's work, focusing on the children, their work, and their ideas. Lillian Katz (1993) observed that teachers often seem reluctant to engage children in meaningful conversations and focus more on giving positive feedback rather than talking about content, relationships, or even what the child is doing.
- Teachers carefully structure their interactions with children to move them forward in concept development through understanding of what Vygotsky (1978) terms the *zone of proximal development.*
- Teachers ensure that all children are able to take part in all facets of the curriculum. In mathematics particularly, equity must be achieved.
- Teachers assess children's attitudes, skills, and knowledge in the area of mathematics using multiple methods. Through observations of children's work and focused discussions with children, teachers plan for indoor and outdoor experiences at the next level of thinking.

SUMMARY

Active children need indoor spaces that are specifically designed to foster active experiences with mathematics. Planning indoor environments begins with making certain the spaces are healthy, safe, beautiful, and accessible to children with special needs. Indoor spaces are arranged with centers of interest, but mathematics is integrated throughout. Centers organize the children's environment, let them see the choices available to them, and give them the means to work and play cooperatively with others.

As Dewey (1938) suggested, the role of the teacher is more complex and more intimate when children are actively engaged in experiential learning. Teachers schedule large blocks of time for children's indoor experiences, and actively teach, guide, observe, focus, and interact with children. No environment is a learning environment without a teacher who is active in planning and encouraging children's concept development.

Active outdoor environments for young children enhance the possibilities for learning in all curricular areas; however, natural surroundings and open spaces are especially important for building active science and math concepts. Well-planned outdoor environments invite inquiry and stimulate children's desire to find the answers to mathematical problems posed by the environment.

A variety of stationary and movable equipment fosters children's physical activity and their understanding of how their bodies move in space. Safety, aesthetics, and balance of environmental factors are taken into consideration when planning for outdoor play and learning. A wide assortment of props and tools aid children in their play and observations.

3

Building Connections to Home and Community Through Active Experiences

The need to understand and be able to use mathematics in everyday life and in the workplace has never been greater and will continue to increase.
　　　　　　　　　　　　　　National Council of Teachers of Mathematics, 2000, p. 4

According to the National Council of Teachers of Mathematics (2000), students, school leaders, parents, the community, and other caregivers share the responsibility to ensure that all students receive a high-quality mathematics education. When all interested parties work together in environments that are equitable, challenging, supportive, and technologically equipped, young children will receive the high-quality mathematics education they will need later in school and as adults. Mathematics helps children make sense of their world outside of school.

John Dewey believed that schools could not function "when separated from the interest of home and community" (Dewey, 1944, p. 86). He depicted the school at the center with the free interplay of influences, materials, and ideas flowing to both the home and the environment around the school building, and back again to life in school. The work of Piaget (Youniss & Damon, 1992) and Vygotsky (Berk & Winsler, 1995) further confirms the importance of building connections to home and community through active experiences.

Vygotsky (1978) saw children as learning to think and develop concepts by mastering challenging tasks in collaboration with more knowledgeable members of their society. In addition to teachers, our communities have many specialists that are available as resources for classes and for individual students. Moreover, many communities have access to science and math centers (Lawrence Hall of Science, Berkeley, California, for example), museums, national laboratories, and industry that can contribute greatly to the understanding of math and encourage students to further their interests outside of school.

Working with others in their school and with the community, teachers will want to build these resources into their interactions with children. Thus, the immediate environment of the school and community serves as a laboratory or workshop in which children discover the world around them and the people and things that populate that world. Without these active experiences, children lack the raw materials to construct learnings in the classroom that have meaning and integrity. Children are cheated when most math concepts are presented to them out of context. According to Basile (1999), one context that has proven beneficial for encouraging development of mathematical concepts and processes is the outdoor environment. Mathematics abounds in nature, and many things found there can be used to teach mathematics in a meaningful and authentic way.

In his ecological approach, Bronfenbrenner (1979) placed the developing child in the center of a series of interlocking settings. Home, school, and the neighborhood serve as the immediate basis for child development and learning. Just as active children derive meaning from their experiences in the classroom, that meaning is extended and broadened when teachers recognize the family and the community as resources for deep and personally meaningful learning experiences.

OUT INTO THE SCHOOL

Now, where can the teacher and children find the active experiences that build connections to home and community and take them outside the classroom walls?

Whether a kindergarten or a Head Start program in a large elementary school, a childcare center or a small cooperative nursery school, there are many meaningful ways to utilize the immediate environment of the building itself or the grounds that surround it.

Inside the School Building

There are many possibilities for active math experiences for children when they take a walk around the school building. Patterns are everywhere in the school building, as are opportunities to measure and compare measurements using traditional and nontraditional tools. Children can count the number of classrooms, tiles on the floor, windows, and doors. They can note where symbols are used and make guesses as to their meanings. When walking through the halls, they are navigating space and applying ideas about direction and distance. "Go right" and "go left" begin to take on meaning as children practice finding their way around the building and look for landmarks and locations.

Maps can be constructed of the school building using both concrete manipulatives and drawings, although it is not expected that they will be true to scale. Children can estimate or hypothesize about what they will find in the building and represent what they find using pictures and graphs. Teachers can create treasure hunts to give children practice in finding their way around the building using various landmarks.

Children are intensely interested in machines and tools that help us do work. Children who are housed in an elementary school setting can meet various school helpers such as the secretary, the nurse, the custodian, and the cook. The teacher might assist the children in making a list of questions to ask by getting them to think about the jobs that people do and what math tools they need to perform their tasks. Children may be asked to speculate what different kinds of tools are used by persons who work in the school, such as thermometers, rulers, scales, containers of various sizes, and word processors. These learnings can be expanded in the classroom as tools are provided for children in various centers of interest.

Outside in the Natural Environment

The immediate outdoor environment of the school provides children with a rich laboratory for studying nature and the physical world as it applies to mathematics. While exploring nature has been viewed mainly as a science activity, opportunities for emergent math skills are abundant. Rocks can be sorted, classified, and ordered by size, number, and other properties. Differences in weight can be estimated, and they may be brought inside for weighing. Spiderwebs and flower petals can be used to study patterns, and trees can be measured around with string and compared as to size (and for older children, age). There are many things to count: "How many baby birds are in that nest?"

Teachers will enjoy finding ways to teach mathematics in a contextual format that is as authentic as possible. Through hands-on manipulation, children discover that some things are heavy and others are light, estimate how many berries are on the bush, and find the pattern on a ladybug. These are math experiences that they will not forget.

OUT INTO THE NEIGHBORHOOD AND COMMUNITY

In planning for meaningful experiences for children, teachers prepare the children, but they also prepare themselves. The purpose of a trip into the neighborhood or community is to provide children with firsthand experiences based on their interests that they would be unable to have in the classroom, in school, or on the immediate grounds. In fact, the first step for the teacher might be to decide if the purpose could be accomplished in any other way. Do the children need to go to the exhibit on shapes at the museum, or would it be possible to bring math resource persons into the school to plan investigations and pose math problems to be answered in a concrete way? If school visits are not possible, or the right people cannot be found, the teacher decides on the goals and then plans for experiences prior to, during, and after the field trip.

Teachers will want to become familiar with the community and its resources prior to planning any trip. Unforeseen difficulties can be avoided if teachers preview the sites and talk with the people at the places they wish to visit. Some sites such as museums and libraries have prepared tours and materials for children; however, these may be too long or complex for very young children. Teachers should shorten and modify an experience when necessary and create their own materials that will be age appropriate.

Teachers will also want to consider the integrative power of a field trip (Seefeldt, 1997). How will the math trip facilitate growth in science, the language arts, literacy, the arts, and social skills? As teachers prepare the children, they will emphasize active experiences in all of these areas. In addition, they will choose children's literature that integrates math throughout the early childhood curriculum. Each active experience will involve learning new vocabulary words and investigating the site through informational books and fiction. Prior to the trip, children may want to make a list of questions that they would like to answer. After the trip, they will want to draw pictures, dictate stories, make charts and graphs, and sing songs about what they have done. They will re-create and reinvent their learnings through dramatic play inside and outside the classroom. Social skills develop as children experience new people and places and acquire behaviors to fit the situation.

BASIC GUIDELINES FOR MEANINGFUL FIELD EXPERIENCES

1. Keep the experience simple for very young children, and increase the complexity as it is developmentally appropriate. For example, very young children will profit from a short walk to look at patterns on historical buildings. With the teacher's help, they may classify the shapes by type. Older children will advance their concepts of shape and pattern by drawing or tracing what they see on the buildings and labeling the shapes and patterns.

2. Consider the mode of transportation. Walking is best for most children, yet some field trips necessitate bus or public transportation. A trip on the bus or metro gives children a chance to compare how long it takes to get there with the time involved to make a walking trip.

3. If the classroom is inclusive, consider all aspects of the field experience. Pathways and sites must be barrier free and experiences must be open-ended so that all children profit from the field trip. Small group excursions may provide a better opportunity for all learners to profit.

4. Introduce the field experience through discussions, pictures, reading about things to be viewed, art experiences, and classroom experiments. For example, if children are to visit the grocery store, provide many books for them (both fiction and nonfiction) about stores and the things they sell. You may want to set up the creative dramatic corner as a grocery store. Children may make pictorial signs with prices for the various items. With the teacher's help, children can make a list of things they wish to purchase, research how much the items cost, and estimate if they have enough money to pay for them. Older children can probably count out money with fair accuracy. Ask questions such as "How many do we need?" "How much do you think the oranges will cost?" "How many oranges are in a dozen?" "How many bananas do you think are in a bunch?" "How heavy do you think the nuts will be?"

5. Organize play around the places to be visited. The creative dramatic center and the outside environment can be adapted to fit math field experiences. Often additional clothes or props will be needed. Boxes and bags can fill the grocery store along with empty cartons, cans, and bins for holding various groceries. Food scales will enhance the experience, as will aprons for the grocers and money for transactions.

6. Prepare the children to observe closely and gather data during the field trip. Their observations will be used as the basis for many activities in the days and weeks to follow. For example, children have probably been to the grocery store with their parents many times. Yet, they have not paid close attention to the patterns, colors, shapes, and variety of goods. For older children, questions may be compiled on sheets before the trip to remind them of the things they wanted to look for.

7. Give children plenty of opportunities to reflect on their experiences. Allot time and materials for follow-up plans and projects. Isolated experiences are easily forgotten. Learnings from field trips are part of an integrated curriculum. Geist (2001) suggests that when children work on projects, a number of opportunities arise for them to use math. In a recent project on construction and transportation, children had an opportunity to use measurement to help them build a truck. They measured how long, tall, and wide they wanted it and then transferred their numbers to the cardboard they were using to make their truck. Their measurements were not totally accurate, but this experience served as a beginning for math learning.

8. Welcome parents during any phase of the planning, implementation, or follow-up. Opportunities for parent participation should accommodate parents' schedules. Parents need not come to the school or field experience. There are many ways they can enhance their children's experiences in the home if they are informed of the teacher's plans and activities.

BUILDING CONNECTIONS WITH THE NEIGHBORHOOD AND COMMUNITY

The National Urban League, in its article "Learning Science and Math in Your Community" (1998), has provided for parents an excellent list of suggestions for places, people, and programs outside the home and school that can add to what parents and teachers provide on a regular basis. These ideas will work for teachers, too, as they build community connections to foster children's skills in mathematics. Every community has natural resources, people resources, and material resources. Teachers and parents will want to

> **SOME SAFETY TIPS FOR FIELD EXPERIENCES**
>
> - Obtain parental permission for children to participate in the excursion.
> - Check the environment ahead, both inside and out, for any hazards.
> - Be sure all teachers and staff members are trained in first aid and CPR.
> - Include at least one person with such training on the trip.
> - Take a first-aid kit on the excursion.
> - Take an up-to-date list of emergency phone numbers for each child.
> - Check medical forms for children's allergies.
> - Always walk on the left, facing traffic.
> - Be sure that children understand what objects are safe to measure. For example, small wild animals are for observation, not handling.
> - Make sure that children do not practice math skills on poisonous plants. Do not allow them to measure the volume of or drink from streams in the outdoor environment.
> - When utilizing transportation, make sure the children know, have practiced, and will follow the rules.
> - Consider the adult/child ratios. Include no more than three or four children on a field trip for each adult present and fewer if the trip requires complex arrangements for transportation.
> - Remember that small group excursions may be best for all learners.
> - Be sure the field trip site meets guidelines for children who are developmentally different.

make an effort to become acquainted with these resources to extend and expand the mathematics offerings possible in the school and the home.

The Neighborhood as a Mathematics Laboratory

On walking excursions, young children do best in small groups. Planning is essential when the trip is known ahead of time. The following criteria provide for experiences with integrity and meaning:

• There is a continuity of experience as one builds upon another. Build experiences around one theme or concept area such as shapes, and help children to construct knowledge in depth and generalize it to other areas.

• Each experience should be worth the child's and teacher's time and effort. A trip to the university math laboratory had been long and exhausting. The exhibits had been placed too high for most young children to see and touch. Worse, the student in charge was not used to young children and lectured them as he did secondary students. The use of the overhead projector could have been instructive, but the children could not see the screen. The children whined, fidgeted, and started poking and fighting with one another. Later, when asked what they remembered about the trip, they talked only about the drinking fountains.

• Advanced organizers should be provided for the children. Young children need opportunities to discuss, read about, and role-play the excursion in advance. Some teachers find that asking children to make a list of what they already know, what they want to see, and what they think they will see on the trip is helpful. Teachers sometimes add the question, "What surprised you about the trip?" After discussing and estimating the sizes of plants in the park, for example, children could compare their original list with what they actually found and recorded in their math journals with the help of the teachers.

• Children should have time to reflect upon and follow up on experiences outside the classroom with plans and projects that enhance and expand their learning. For example, on a trip to a construction site, the children estimated how tall the buildings were and which were longer and taller. When they returned to the classroom, they used the block area to construct their own site and used standard and nonstandard measures to chart and compare their "hands-on" block buildings. They also began to think about "how big" the other buildings would have to be.

• A planned experience should either be an outgrowth of children's deep interests or meet a specific need for the children in learning subject matter content. Mrs. Porter's class became very interested in the patterns and shapes they observed in art and in the classroom itself. They were excited when their teacher extended their experiences to patterns found in nature, which they drew and described in stories, and patterns found in houses and buildings.

• Flexibility is essential. While most outside experiences are well planned in advance, teachers should capitalize on incidental learnings, such as when children ponder "How many cars are going through that busy intersection?" This question leads to many more and gives teachers the opportunity to utilize all areas of the math curriculum for young children.

Other Neighborhood Resources

• Local businesses. Teachers need to make sure that there are people who are knowledgeable about how math is used in their business and like to talk to young children. It would be nice if hands-on experiences are available as well. A restaurant or small store is a good place to learn the basic concept of money. Young children love buying and selling, although they confuse the size of the money with how much it is worth and have difficulty conserving. Yet, with the teacher's help, they can make a grocery list, count out money, and go to the store to buy the ingredients for a cooking project or a party. They can also be allocated an amount to buy lunch at a neighborhood restaurant and make sure they do not spend more than they have.

Older elementary children may be interested in how much it costs the restaurant to buy the food and pay the employees. They might even be able to make some estimate about how much money the owner can make given the prices of the food.

• Buildings and houses in the community. These can create a lot of math activities. Young children can draw simple plans for buildings, copy a building with large or small blocks, and count windows or the number of floors. Older children can estimate and measure windows, doors, and stairs.

• Maps. Making and using maps involves measurement and geometry. Young children can make simple maps of their rooms at home. As they get older, they can choose shapes to represent furniture, windows, or doors. This is the beginning of symbolic representation. The National Urban League (1998) suggests that making a map of the neighborhood can be a great family or school project for older children. At the same time that children learn math, they learn more about what is in their neighborhood.

• Science centers and museums. They have planned activities for children including experiments and opportunities to use technology that small preschools cannot afford.

At the Lawrence Hall of Science in Berkeley, California, there is a program in Family Math where families work together on math concepts and problems. Family Math has been expanded to other areas of the country as well. At the Smithsonian Institution in Washington, D.C., "Don't Touch" has been replaced by "Please Touch with Care" in the discovery and interactive computer areas of the museum. Trained personnel supervise the handling of fragile equipment.

Other community resources that teachers may want to consider are

    colleges and universities

    radio or television stations

    professional services such as doctors' offices and hospitals

    commercial services such as bakeries, pharmacies, factories, and farms

    children's museums with hands-on exhibits

Visitors who enhance the math curriculum include parents and other specialists in computer technologies, music, art, cooking, mechanics, and many other fields that have mathematics aspects. They can be effective resource people if the teacher prepares the children carefully for their visits, and encourages them to provide active demonstrations or hands-on opportunities. Women visitors who are involved in mathematics build a sense in young children that math is not just a male endeavor.

THE HOME-SCHOOL CONNECTION

> Parents (including, for our purposes in this paper, adult family members and other caregivers), especially of young children, want to be involved in their children's education. Their ideas of how to help usually include reading to their children, helping them learn the alphabet, and teaching them how to count. Frequently, however, parents don't know how to go beyond these activities, especially in mathematics. (Davila Coates & Thompson, 1999, p. 205)

Classrooms work best and children learn more when parents are involved. The joint position statement of the National Association for the Education of Young Children and the National Council for Teachers of Mathematics (2002) suggests public campaigns to build awareness of families' central role in mathematical development. Also possible is the distribution of materials in ways similar to those of reading initiatives and computer-linked as well as school-based meetings for families. Teachers may employ the following multiple approaches, as well as modeling some of their strategies from the Family Math program, which has worked since 1981 to involve parents and caregivers of kindergarten to eighth-grade children in their mathematics education.

    • Conferences in which teachers provide parents with samples of children's work and invite parents to share their observations about their children's learning and their suggestions for classroom and community experience based on their children's interests.

    • Meetings and workshops that counter the idea that math is not interesting or that parents cannot master math concepts. Family Math found that a huge number of adults had inaccurate concepts of what math teaching was all about and felt at a loss to begin to work on math concepts with their children. Some of the ideas that follow will assist teachers in giving parents the confidence to do math with their children. Additionally, math can be taught in the child's (and parent's) native language. Many math books for children are now translated into Spanish and other languages, including *The Doorbell Rang (Llaman a la Puerta)* by P. Hutchins and *Moja Means One: Swahili Counting Book* by Muriel Feelings.

- Informal contacts. Busy parents enjoy a brief chat before school, telephone calls, informal notes, and bulletin boards and exhibits that inform them of plans and programs and invite them to participate in a variety of ways.

- Somewhat more formal contacts through the provision of a Parents' Corner or Family Room where parents may interact around math learning materials, reference books, children's literature based on math, and other activities of interest to the family. Often these items may be checked out by family members.

- Regular newsletters explaining the goals for the week, why certain activities were planned, and how parents can support the lessons at home. Each active experience in the later part of this book has a section that explains what parents can do in an informal way to support children's emergent concept development in the area of math. Other items to include in newsletters are special events at school, math activities and puzzles that children have enjoyed, special television programs on topics of math that parents and children might watch together, and special events for children and families occurring in the community.

- An open-door policy for parent observation and participation. If parents are unable to work regularly as paid or unpaid volunteers, they may make or send materials for special projects in the classroom, help on field experiences, or come to school when their schedules permit.

- Parties and meetings such as Family Math Nights where parents may have an opportunity to ask questions and have hands-on experiences themselves with the math curriculum being used in the classroom. One of the goals of the Family Math program is to get families talking together about mathematical ideas and doing activities that sometimes involve informal learning centers.

- Active science experiences for children that can be documented for parents. Children will have products such as drawings, charts, or stories to communicate to busy parents what they are doing in school.

Parents can encourage mathematical thinking in their children by asking open-ended questions and taking time to encourage the answers. They can help their children to observe ("What shapes do you see on that tree?"), classify ("Let's put away your toys by color"), estimate ("How long will it take that squirrel to get up the tree?"), and quantify ("How tall is that building?"). It is possible to practice the skills of mathematics everywhere.

Teachers will want to plan family math events at school and send suggestions home in the class newsletter for supporting math learning in the home such as a simple recipe that involves the measurement of volume. Successful school math events will involve the whole family in collecting data, undertaking the investigation of problems, and solving math puzzles. These are active experiences for the whole family. The standard school math fair usually involves complex materials and equipment and seems more like a competition than a joint exploration that is both fun and intellectually stimulating. Also, when children and parents work together on math, parents learn math too.

The following interactions with parents should introduce them to, and involve them in, children's mathematics experiences:

1. In the class newsletter, have a weekly suggestion box designed for supplementing the math curriculum at home. For example, highlight free activities occurring in the community such as children's math book programs at libraries or bookstores, exhibits to be visited, and activities based on kitchen and gardening math.

2. Have parents and children work together to create exhibits at home that can be shared with the class when completed. Send parents a note explaining the goal of an activity, how it is related to work at school, and simple suggestions. An example might be drawings of animals using only geometric shapes.

3. Put together a "math backpack" that children take home on a rotating basis. The backpack contains a note explaining the purpose of the activity, an information book related to the activity, and all the materials necessary for completing the activity. The teacher will want to make sure that all of the materials contained in the backpack are easy and fun for parents and children to use and translated into their native language.

Additionally, even if family members cannot volunteer in the classroom on a regular basis, they can share their talents, occupations, hobbies, customs, and traditions with the class and school community as they are able. Juan's father loved to build furniture. He shared his talents with the class, demonstrating how he used standard measuring tools. The children understood that math is important in all endeavors.

SUMMARY

According to Davila Coates and Thompson (1999), working with community members and using community settings are often effective ways of reaching parents who have traditionally been alienated from the schools. Libraries, community centers, and community-based organizations can serve as alternative venues. Whether in school or in an alternative setting, creating a friendly, nonthreatening atmosphere is necessary. Choosing mathematics activities that parents recognize as important to them is also very significant in getting parents to buy into the math program.

Presenting activities in the home language will reach parents whose first language is not English. When it is not possible to make translations, try parents, older siblings, and community members as helpers. According to Weaver and Gaines (1999), the most obvious way to incorporate the child's first language into the classroom is to enlist the help of a person fluent in that language. In addition, the children's home culture should be incorporated into the classroom. Using children's books set in the children's culture is one way to do this. An example is *The Bicycle Man* (1982) by Allen Say. In the context of a sports event, Japanese children learn how many measurement skills are necessary to make judgments.

Building and maintaining connections with home and community provide benefits to all. Young children need active experiences consistent with their participation in mathematics education. These experiences require careful planning by teachers, who are rewarded by observing children's authentic learning, as one experience builds upon another into an integrated whole. As the family is recognized as a valuable resource for learning, parents and teachers feel mutually supported and learn to understand and value each other as contributors to the child's understanding of mathematics. All of this is consistent with a strong emphasis on mathematics in the curriculum for young children.

4

Experiences and Mathematical Content

Experiences in order to be educative, must lead out into an expanding world of subject-matter.

John Dewey, 1938, p. 37

Firsthand experiences in their classrooms, homes, and communities form the foundation for children's math learning. Children gain mathematical knowledge as they notice that they are taller or shorter than another or that their friend has more Hot Wheels cars than they do, or while they grapple with the problem of how to balance a block tower or share a plate of cookies.

These informal ideas of math, however, are like the first rungs on the learning ladder. They help children make sense of their world and help them construct a solid foundation for success in school (NCTM & NAEYC, 2002). But unless a firsthand experience leads children to an ever-expanding world of new facts, information, and knowledge previously unfamiliar, children's mathematical learning will be limited to the informal. Thus, the next step on the learning ladder is the expansion and extension of the knowledge children have gained through their firsthand experiences into a fuller, richer, thicker, and more organized form (Dewey, 1938; NCTM & NAEYC, 2002). This form gradually approximates the experts' understanding of mathematics.

Teachers who enable children to turn their direct, firsthand experiences with their world into a coherent, organized body of mathematical knowledge are the double specialists Piaget (1970) wrote of. These are teachers who are engrossed in knowledge of each individual child—what each child knows, how each one learns—and who also have knowledge of the subject matter of mathematics. Then, because teachers are double specialists, they know how to bring children and subject matter content together.

KNOWLEDGE OF CHILDREN

Knowledge of children's understanding of mathematical concepts is necessary. There will be wide variation in children's understanding of mathematical concepts. Some of this variation is due to the sociocultural context of children's lives, and some to the variation in patterns of normal growth and development. Even though individual children develop differently, research and theory inform us about how children develop concepts of mathematics.

Jean Piaget (1969) studied children's thinking and their concepts of number. He outlined the development of number concepts in children, tracing the beginning of number concepts from birth at the sensorimotor stage through formal operations at around age 11 or 12.

Sensorimotor (Birth–2)

Piaget's observations of children suggest that infants come into the world with only a few reflex actions—cooing, sucking, and moving the tongue. Through their actions on the environment and the sensations they receive, they begin to impose organization or structure on what they do. Concepts of mathematics are believed to develop as children grasp small and large objects, touch a variety of blocks, or move objects of different shapes around the floor.

Piaget believed that mathematical understandings begin when infants develop object permanence, the realization that an object exists even if they are not present. When children can think about something not in their environment, they can use symbols, imitate, and use words to represent objects.

Preoperational (2–7/8)

The preoperational stage of thought and mathematical knowledge is characterized by the development of preconcepts. Children begin to develop the ability to internalize objects and events and relate these by their common properties. In other words, they develop ideas or concepts about their world. But these concepts or ideas are not like those of an adult. They are referred to as preconcepts, or embryonic concepts, the beginning or foundation of later, more complex, complete, and accurate ideas.

Children in the preoperational stage begin to manipulate symbols or representations of the physical world. They begin to conserve, which is necessary for all later mathematical understanding. Without the ability to conserve, children may be able to learn simple mathematical skills or routine calculations, but they will be constrained in developing mathematical understandings and will be unable to solve more complex problems or tasks.

There are three levels of conservation.

1. Children consider it natural for the form or number of materials to change or vary according to their arrangement, shape, or the container they are in.

2. Children develop the idea that the amount of matter stays the same even if arranged differently.

3. Children are able to conserve quantities, volume, discontinuous quantities, and mass. They will tell you, "It's still the same—you just moved them around." Or "You didn't take any away or add any; you only put them closer together."

Through the preschool years, children's mathematical thinking is called semilogical. Because they can't keep in mind more than one relationship at a time, they have difficulty making comparisons and seeing relationships. They are unable to use the reversible thought processes that would permit them to think logically.

This tells us that, in general, the younger the child the more wedded the child is to learning through firsthand interactions with the environment and others. Three-, four-, and five-year olds, still in the preoperational period of cognitive development, must rely on firsthand experiences in order to construct their own knowledge and learn. As they grow and mature, however, they become increasingly reliant on learning through symbols, through pictures, and through spoken and written language.

There are many resources teachers can use to gain a better understanding of children's mathematical as well as general growth and development. Authorities in the field of early childhood, such as Gesell, Ilg, and Ames, whose studies were reported in *Infant and Child in the Culture of Today* (1974), and Sue Bredekamp and Carol Copple, who wrote *Developmentally Appropriate Practice in Early Childhood Programs* (1997), have identified universal patterns of children's growth, development, and learning.

KNOWLEDGE OF THE SUBJECT MATTER—MATHEMATICS

Knowledge of children alone is not enough. If teachers are to take children further up the learning ladder, then they must also have a solid understanding of the subject matter they want children to learn.

Just as authorities in the field of early childhood have identified universals of children's growth, development, and learning, so have authorities in the field of mathematics identified general facts, information, and knowledge key to mathematics (NCTM, 2001). Knowledge of these key concepts or themes that serve to organize mathematical content guides teachers in the selection of firsthand experiences that will serve as a base for children's learning, as well as leads children in expanding and extending these firsthand experiences into more formal, conventional knowledge.

The National Council of Teachers of Mathematics (1989; 2001) has established principles for teaching mathematics to young children. These principles of learning are embedded in the standards and follow here:

> *Equity.* The idea that all children and their families hold high expectations for children's mathematical learning and that these expectations are fulfilled through strong support, curriculum, and programs for all our nation's children.
>
> *Curriculum.* Teachers understand that mathematics learning is not a series of isolated one-time activities, but rather is a coherent, focused, and well-articulated program that continues from early childhood through the grades (NCTM & NAEYC, 2002).
>
> *Teaching.* Knowing mathematics means "doing mathematics." "A person gathers, discovers, or creates knowledge in the course of some activity having a purpose" (NCTM, 1989, p. 7). Thus teaching and learning mathematics, not just for young children but for adults as well, emphasize firsthand experiences that involve students in meaningful, purposeful, activity.
>
> *Technology.* With the advent of the computer and other technology, many aspects of doing mathematics have changed in the last decade. This does not mean, however, that children do not need opportunities to develop an understanding of mathematical models, structures, and simulations applicable to many disciplines.
>
> The mathematics program in early childhood should take advantage of technology. With teachers' guidance, children should learn when the use of a calculator is appropriate. Every child should also have access to a computer for individual and group work. Guided work using a computer, which can benefit all children, is especially helpful for those with physical limitations.
>
> *Learning.* Most mathematical knowledge is not social knowledge, not something that can be told to children. Piaget (1969) demonstrated that children construct their own knowledge through their social, mental, and physical activities.
>
> To foster children's construction of mathematics knowledge, teachers will need to determine what children already know about mathematics and what they still have to learn. Children's development of number sense should move through increasingly sophisticated levels of constructing ideas and skills.
>
> Time, appropriate materials, and interaction with others are necessary to support children's engagement in mathematic ideas. Play is the way children can pursue their own purposes and tackle problems that are challenging and yet within their own capabilities (NCTM & NAEYC, 2002).
>
> Mathematics is integrated with other learning activities, and other learning activities are integrated with mathematics. Everyday routines, for instance, involve

children in mathematical concepts. Children may count the days until a special event by removing rings on a paper chain or marking the days on a calendar. Or they may count the children allowed at the woodworking table at a given time and, while working with wood, use arbitrary measurements to achieve their goal.

Problem Solving. Focus on problem solving. Problem solving and reasoning are the heart of mathematics (NCTM & NAEYC, 2002). Thus children are encouraged to observe, question, collect information, communicate ideas, make connections and representations, and reflect on their experiences.

Assessment. Assessment, teaching, and learning are one and the same. Authentic assessment is a part of the curriculum. As children build with blocks, teachers note their use of descriptive shape words. Or children are asked to count the number of children needed to play a game, and their knowledge of counting is observed and recorded.

THE STANDARDS

The standards the National Council of Teachers of Mathematics has delineated are not separate topics or themes, but are interwoven strands designed to support the learning of meaningful mathematics.

1. *Number and Operation*

    At the heart of mathematics is an understanding of numbers. Children need to be able to make sense of the ways numbers are used in their everyday world (NCTM, 1989). They will begin counting, and as they mature and have increasingly sophisticated experiences, they will count with understanding, knowing that when they count four objects, four is the number of objects they have.

    Children will begin to find ways of representing numbers. They may make marks, or begin to recognize and write numerals. By age 5 or 6, children should begin to develop an understanding of what numerals stand for.

    Children will also begin to understand the meanings of number operations and how they relate to one another. Involved in real-life experiences, children begin to ask questions about number operations: "How many are left?" "How many more do we need?" "How many did you add?"

2. *Geometry and Spatial Awareness*

    Geometry is another area of particular importance in the curriculum for 3- to 6-year-olds. Young children's natural awareness of shapes and their play with shapes can be expanded into learning the vocabulary of shapes, and being able to identify and describe the attributes of a variety of shapes.

    Geometry also involves spatial awareness and understanding. To develop spatial awareness, children need to investigate, experiment, and explore everyday objects and physical materials. They need to feel themselves in space, climbing high, swinging low, crawling in and out of objects, on top of and under other objects. As children do so, teachers introduce them to the vocabulary of space, question them about their position in space, and help them relate ideas of shapes and space to number concepts and measurement.

3. *Measurement*

   Measurement is a powerful mathematic tool. As geometry, introducing concepts of measurement seems natural in good schools for young children. Before children can understand measurable attributes, they must have firsthand experiences using arbitrary tools to measure things and spaces in their world. From this background children will find needs for conventional measurement.

4. *Patterns and Relationships*

   A component of algebra, patterning, "merits special mention because it is accessible and interesting to young children" (NCTM & NAEYC, 2002, p. 9). Being able to recognize, describe, and create patterns grows to undergird algebraic thinking, and supports the development of number sense, spatial sense, and other conceptual areas.

   Pattern recognition involves all kinds of things. Children can begin to notice patterns in the routine of the day, or patterns of colors, shapes, or sizes. Being able to recognize patterns leads to recognizing a variety of relationships in patterns, which in turn leads to making mathematical connections (NCTM, 1989).

5. *Data Description, Organization, Representation, and Analysis*

   Active children learn through active experiences. Real-life experiences directly lead into organizing, representing, and displaying information. Children make graphs of their findings, draw and paint pictures to represent their work, discuss problems encountered, and reach conclusions.

6. *Problem Solving*

   Young children seem driven to solve problems. They explore and examine their world—tasting, taking things apart, pulling, pushing—all in an attempt to find out how it works. This natural drive to solve problems is built on in the mathematics program. Teachers make certain children will encounter many real-life mathematical problems. These will arise from both real-world and mathematical contexts (NCTM, 1989). For instance, children will need to count the number of cups of flour they use to make bread, the number of children they need to play a game, or the number of children who can work at the wood table at one time.

BRINGING KNOWLEDGE OF CHILDREN AND MATHEMATICS TOGETHER

To bring children and mathematics together, teachers first need to find out all they can about the content of mathematics. To do so, they might

- reread their math textbooks from high school or college. Without a solid understanding of mathematics, teachers are limited in helping children see and understand relationships, or make connections between numbers, measurement, and other areas of mathematics.

- ask authorities in mathematics. Perhaps a high school student or teacher could explain the connections between understanding and recognizing patterns and later understanding of algebra. Search the Web or attend lectures on teaching mathematics to young children.
- talk with primary-grade teachers to find out what understanding of mathematics children learn while in the primary grades and how to best build children's foundational knowledge of these areas.

Once teachers have a solid understanding of mathematics, they will want to find out what children already know and understand about mathematical concepts. To do so, teachers can

- interview children. If you want to introduce children to counting, informally ask them to count objects for you, or to count as high as they can.
- ask children to tell you all they know about a specific topic. For example, if you want to develop children's concepts of shapes, you might ask individuals to tell you all they know about shapes, or to draw, paint, or dance shapes.
- talk with children's families. Ask about family goals for children's mathematical learning and what number experiences the child is interested in and likes doing, is not familiar with, or needs to become familiar with.
- observe children as they work and play. Note how they use number concepts and ideas and how they solve mathematical programs, use their mathematical language, and interact with others using math concepts.

EXPANDING AND EXTENDING FIRSTHAND EXPERIENCES

Children's experiences with their world enable them to develop spontaneous, informal mathematical ideas. This everyday, personal knowledge, however, does not automatically lead to a deeper understanding or more conventional way of knowing. Rather these concepts act like Velcro, hooking onto whatever new information, facts, and experiences children are given. The richer the new information, the greater the possibility for children to see the relationship between one math fact and another, and to form generalizations.

Vygotsky (1986) pointed out that at different developmental stages, children learn different things as they independently act on and interpret their environment, but also other people interact with children, affecting the course of their development and learning. He thought children operate at two levels of thought. One is the stage at which they can solve problems and think without the guidance of an adult or a more skilled peer. The second level is when the child can do the same task with adult help or guidance. He called this the potential developmental level. The distance between the two levels was termed the "zone of proximal development" (Vygotsky, 1986).

This means that by understanding children's existing ideas and the content of mathematics, teachers can extend and expand children's knowledge by

- providing children with all kinds of books—poetry, literature, single-concept, picture, and reference books—that pertain to the mathematics standards and concepts. Books may be openly displayed on a shelf or table, inviting children to extend and expand their ideas of a given concept. Children can use some books independently; others you will want to read to the entire group or to an individual child or two.

- showing children how they can use number operations to solve problems. Working collaboratively with children, teachers can demonstrate how to cut paper in half, share a plate of cookies so each child has one cookie, set a table with one plate, napkin and glass at each place, or cut a pizza into eighths.
- telling children the names of numerals. Knowing the names of numerals is social knowledge. Social knowledge is different from abstract knowledge (Piaget, 1969). Social knowledge—for example, the name of this figure is five, and it stands for five things, count five blocks; or this numeral is four, and it means there are four things—is simply told to children. There is no way for them to construct it for themselves.
- questioning children. Asking children questions can spur their thinking in a new, different, or more conventional way. Asking how many they have, what would happen if they took two away, why they made the pattern in the way they did, how they got so many pieces, and so on can lead children to thinking about their actions.
- having children use the computer to practice a number skill, learn a new skill or fact, find information, or communicate with others.
- using the language of mathematics. Introduce words such as *more than, less than, fewer, taller, first, last,* and so on.
- adding another experience. Based on your understanding of children's ideas and concepts of mathematics, add another real-life experience that will expand and extend these.
- providing multiple opportunities for children to learn from one another.

Children should be able to revisit their existing ideas of mathematics by freely sharing their view of the world with others and arguing their point of view. Only through interactions with others can children critically consider their existing ideas, and revise these to form more complex and conventional concepts of their world.

Respecting children, how they learn, and the subject matter, teachers extend and expand children's existing knowledge. Teachers teach. Bredekamp and Rosegrant (1995) ask teachers "not to water down the learning experience even for the youngest child" (p. 22), but rather to build on children's existing knowledge and experience, assessing and supporting learning.

SUMMARY

Firsthand experiences enable children to construct everyday, spontaneous mathematics concepts. These concepts are like the first rung on a ladder of learning. The role of the teacher is to extend and expand these concepts into fuller, richer, more conventional knowledge. Teachers do this by developing an understanding of children and how they learn and a knowledge of content, and then bringing the two together.

Authorities in the field of mathematics have identified themes or concepts key to the field. These are used by teachers to guide them as they extend and expand children's everyday concepts.

Concepts can be expanded and extended in a number of ways. Books, print media, the computer, and other technologies can be made available. Teachers can demonstrate

Chapter 4 ◆ Experiences and Mathematical Content

skills or apply concepts, and give children information that will enable them to reach a fuller understanding of themselves and the world in which they live. Below is a checklist to assist teachers in picking quality mathematics books for young children.

Checklist for Choosing Mathematics Books for Young Children

- Is it a good book? Would I read this book to the children even if I weren't choosing it for a math lesson?
- Does the book stimulate curiosity? Will the children be inspired to do their own authentic investigations as a result of reading this book?
- Can the children make connections with the book? Are they familiar with some concepts so they can "launch" from there?
- Is the book contrived or are the math connections a natural part of the story or nonfictional presentation?
- Is the information accurate?
- Does the author use interesting details?
- Does the author acknowledge expert advisors?
- Is the book well organized with a clear structure?
- Is it easy to find information?
- Are there useful features such as an index, a table of contents, a glossary, and suggestions for other books and resources on the topic?
- Does the book have an appealing layout and design?
- Do photographs, diagrams, graphics, and other illustrations add to, explain, and extend information?
- Can the content and the language be understood by the intended audience?

PART TWO

Guides to Active Experiences

Experience 1

Young Children Develop Ideas of Number and Counting

FOR THE TEACHER

◇ What You'll Need to Know

"I can count to 10," says 3-year-old Darnella. "Listen to me," she continues. "One, two, four, five, ten." During the period of infancy and toddlerhood, children begin developing mathematical skills, concepts, and misconceptions of number (NRC, 2001). By age 2, children are counting from one to ten for a specific purpose, such as to chant counting songs such as "Ten in the Bed," and often just for fun. This early counting has several characteristics and meanings. As Darnella demonstrated, much of what children know of number involves counting as well as making frequent mistakes and missing portions in the counting sequence (Baroody & Wilkins, 1999; NRC, 2001).

Because children count fingers and buttons, and sign and chant finger plays involving counting to ten, adults may think that early counting is a simple process for them. Yet, young children's counting is not simple, but a highly complex process. Counting involves thinking, perception, and movement (NRC, 2001). To be able to count, children must think, "What is being counted? Which things are not being counted?" They then have to pair the item they are counting with a number name, and finally children understand that the number they say represents the number of objects they have counted.

Even though young children like Darnella demonstrate their conceptual and procedural knowledge of number through counting, they generally do not have an understanding of quantity. Children under age 5 usually cannot tell you what number comes before or after another. Nor does counting early mean children have an understanding of one-to-one correspondence. They can't match the numbers they are saying to the objects the numbers represent. It doesn't seem to bother them that there are 8 buttons and they've counted 10 (Copley, 2000).

When 2- or 3-year-old children are given six chips and asked to count the chips, they might say, "One, two, three, four, five, six, seven, eight, nine, ten." Having memorized the order and names of the numerals, very young children can recite the numbers, but often count some of the chips more than once, or miss counting other chips. These children do not have an awareness of the fact that they are paring the term "one" with the first object they are counting, the term "two" with the second, and so on.

Counting becomes more solidified for 5-year-olds. An example of rational counting is a child who says, "I'm not five yet. I'm this many," and counts four fingers, saying "One, two, three, four! I'm four. Then I'll be five. It's this many," and holding up five fingers. Or a child who counts the buttons on her coat. "One, two, three, four, five," she says. "I have five buttons on my coat." To count rationally, children must have an underlying idea of logico-mathematical knowledge. When children count rationally, they have constructed a mental structure of number and have assimilated number words into this structure. Now counting has become a rational tool for children to use when counting and solving problems.

Because counting, which seems natural to young children, is essential to all other number operations, teachers deliberately foster counting in the early childhood curriculum. They do so by providing opportunities for children to learn the names of the numerals. More importantly, however, teachers structure the environment and curriculum in ways that put children face-to-face with problems that call for them to construct their own knowledge of number.

◇ Key Concepts

- Counting involves learning the vocabulary of mathematics, including knowing the names of the numerals.
- Counting involves the ability to understand one-to-one correspondence.

Experience 1 ◆ Young Children Develop Ideas of Number and Counting

- Counting involves the ability to understand cardinality: that the last number word said when counting a group of objects, such as two, represents two things, objects, events, and so on.
- Counting involves saying number words in a consistent, reproducible order.
- Counting involves abstraction; any thing can be collected together for counting.
- Counting involves the understanding that things can be counted in any sequence without changing the result.
- Counting leads to experiencing the number operations of adding and taking away.

◇ Goals and Objectives

Research shows there are great variations in children's abilities to count (NRC, 2001). Early childhood educators will consider these individual differences as they select goals for children's counting experiences.

Children will develop the disposition to count and use numbers in their everyday activities and experiences.

Children will learn the names of numerals, and 5-year-olds will begin to write them.

Children will be able to count sequentially.

Children will have meaningful experiences counting to find out the quantity of items.

Children will have meaningful opportunities to count using one-to-one correspondence.

Children will begin to use number operations in their everyday experiences.

◇ What You'll Need

The following books can enhance early educators' knowledge and understanding of children's developing ability to count and how to best foster children's procedural and conceptual knowledge of number and counting.

Copley, J. V. (2000). *The young child and mathematics.* Washington, DC: National Association for the Education of Young Children.

National Research Council. (2001). *Adding it up: Helping children learn mathematics.* J. Kilpatrick, J. Swafford, & B. Findell (Eds.). Mathematics Learning Study Committee, Center for Education, Division of Behavioral and Social Sciences and Education. Washington, DC: National Academy Press.

Stanmark, J. K., Thompson, V., & Cossey, R. (1986). *Family math.* New York: Equals.

Children's Books

Literally, there are thousands and thousands of counting books. The following meet the criteria for good children's literature as well as introduce children to number and counting.

Ehlert, L. (2001). *Fish eyes: A book you can count on.* New York: Harcourt Brace.

Gerth, M. (2001). *Ten little ladybugs.* New York: Piggy Toes Press.

Grossman, V. (1998). *Ten little rabbits.* New York: Chronicle Books.

Keats, J. E. (1999). *Over in the meadow.* New York: Puffin.

Wood, J. (1992). *Moo, moo, brown cow.* New York: Gulliver Books.

Other Things You'll Need

- Counting chips
- A variety of materials for children to handle and count
- A counting table complete with sorting boards and a variety of materials for children to count
- Plastic, magnetic, wooden, flannel board, or other numbers for children to handle and sort
- Board games such as Candy Land, bingo, and others
- Sand and water play areas, complete with containers and tools for children to use to count as they play
- Handheld calculators, calendars, receipt books, cell phones, and other counting supplies in the housekeeping area

◇ **The Home-School Connection**

Learning to count takes place everywhere—at home, during children's play in a park, at the supermarket, in the childcare center, actually everywhere children are. Thus, building the home-school connection enhances children's opportunities to count and learn to use numbers with meaning. Remind parents that they can foster children's counting.

1. Send home copies of counting poems and songs children sing/chant at school so parents can sing/chant these with their children.

2. Arrange for counting books to be available for children to take home to "read" with their parents.

3. Send home newsletters about how children learn to count rationally through everyday experiences such as setting a table, putting a sock and shoe on each foot, counting how many cookies they'll need for each of their friends to have one, and so on. Sample newsletters are on the tear-out sheets at the end of this experience (pp. 65–67).

4. Hold a workshop on mathematical learning for children. During the workshop, demonstrate how children use parquet blocks, blocks, and other small manipulatives to count. (See the tear-out sheet on page 68.)

5. At the end of the workshop, give parents copies of *More Than 1, 2, 3-*, written by Janet McCracken and published by the National Association for the Education of Young Children. These are $10 for 100 copies.

◇ **Evaluating and Assessing Children's Learning**

Just as children naturally count throughout their day, teachers naturally evaluate and assess children's knowledge and understanding of counting. They observe children using

Experience 1 ◆ Young Children Develop Ideas of Number and Counting

numbers, question them, and challenge children by presenting problems and observing how they solve them.

As each child will construct his or her own knowledge of counting, individual evaluation of children's counting abilities is called for. Work with individual children in the following ways:

- Modeling after Piaget, interview each child individually. Put out a number of chips on a table in an irregular pattern and ask children to tell you how many chips there are and then to place the same amount on the table. Children just beginning to construct knowledge of number will not even understand the directions. At the next level children will make a rough copy of the way the chips are arranged on the table. Then they'll methodically look at the model and copy it, using fingers to point at the corresponding elements each time, and when they've achieved concepts of number, they will count the number in the model and count the same number of chips.

- Continue interviewing children for different purposes. You might ask them to count the chips on the table, to show you a big chip or a smaller chip, or to show specific numerals.

- Observe children as they use counting and numbers in their play. Record the observations and place in children's portfolios.

FOR THE CHILDREN

1. Children Will Develop the Disposition to Count and Use Mathematical Concepts in Their Everyday Lives

    ◆ One of the goals of the preschool experience is to have children fall in love with math. This doesn't mean that everything is fun for children, but rather that children use and enjoy the use of numbers and mathematical concepts throughout the day in meaningful ways. It means that children's natural curiosity and openness to explore a wide variety of mathematical ideas is fostered within the context of their real world (NCTM, 1998).

    Children's beliefs in themselves and their ability to use numbers also have a great influence on their thinking and performance. Children who are successful in mathematics seem to love math. These children believe they can learn mathematical concepts, and because they hold this belief, they are more motivated to put the time and effort into learning mathematics (Galper, Wigfield, & Seefeldt, 1997).

    Thus, the role of the early childhood educator is to foster children's natural inclination to count, promote each child's success with numbers, and provide them with meaningful firsthand experiences with numbers.

    - Have board games available that involve counting such as Candy Land and others. Make up card games; play Go Fish and other games. With small groups of children play bingo.

    - Set up a counting table. On it place counting boards made of clear plastic cups glued on a heavy piece of cardboard or ply board. Or provide clear plastic boxes divided into sections, plastic glasses, and other containers.

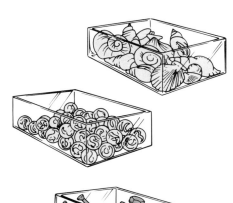

- Provide children with a variety of manipulatives for counting and sorting. In clear plastic containers you could supply
  - seashells, leaves, acorns, pine cones, rocks, jewels (sparkling stones).
  - large buttons that can't be stuffed in any body opening.
  - large marbles of different colors and types.
  - small unbreakable doll dishes, small teddy bears, and so on.
  - nuts and bolts, screws.
  - pieces of plastic pipes and joiners.
  - a box of different types of bells—cow, decorative, sleigh—to listen to and count.
  - a box of discarded greeting cards—from Valentine's Day, Hanukkah, Christmas—or other cards to count and sort by type.
  - plastic or wooden animals, dinosaurs, birds, zoo animals, farm animals, trains, cars, or trucks to play with, count, and sort.
  - wristwatches. A teacher of 4-year-olds asked parents to send in their discarded wristwatches. The children first played with the watches, putting them on and taking them off as they pretended to go to work or as they played house. Children began categorizing the watches by the type of band—leather, metal, and so on. One of the children noticed that some of the watches had numerals on the face and others did not, and children counted the watches with and without numerals.
  - small doll dishes, cups, and saucers. Too small to really use in the dramatic play area, these toys are fun to count and sort.
  - balancing scales. Another teacher obtained a couple of balancing scales, and the children began counting how many acorns it took to balance a unit block on the scales. They continued by counting the number of seashells that would balance a book, a doll, and so on.

◆ Opportunities for learning mathematics and counting should be positive and supportive. "Children must learn to trust their own abilities to make sense of mathematics" (NCTM, 2001, p. 2). Teachers of young children can support children's developing counting skills.
  - Provide children with different types of blocks—unit, parquet, and hollow—and the time and freedom to build and play with these in their own way. As children play, teachers observe and find ways to extend, expand, and build on children's existing knowledge of mathematics and counting. Teachers might
    - count the number of unit blocks in a child's roadway.
    - ask how two blocks are the same or different.
    - place a basket of blocks next to the balance scale, put a unit block on one side of the scale, and ask children to find blocks that balance the scale.
    - ask children how many blocks tall a building is.
    - count the number of round, triangle, or other shaped blocks.

Experience 1 ◆ Young Children Develop Ideas of Number and Counting

Provide children a variety of things to count, move around, and sort.

- Think of the opportunities for mathematical concepts and counting in sand and water areas. All young children enjoy playing with sand and water. These "fill and spill" activities give children opportunities to find out what water and sand are like, as well as introduce children to the idea that matter stays the same even if in different sizes and types of containers. Children will need to be cognitively mature to realize this; however, by playing with water and filling and emptying a three-dimensional space, children are actually experiencing volume and weight.

  Provide children with all types of containers—pipes, sieves, pitchers, cups, boxes, plastic bottles, and slotted and other types of spoons. Clear containers let children see the level of sand or water inside. As they play, ask children to

  - count the number of cups of sand or water needed to fill a larger container
  - make enough sand cakes for children playing in the sand area
  - build a sand castle taller than a bucket

- Add counting materials to the dramatic play area or areas. For example, add pretend coins and bills to wallets and purses to foster children's counting while shopping. Or you could add

  - cellular or other phones to dial
  - handheld calculators that actually work
  - register receipts
  - receipt books to fill in
  - nonactive checkbooks
  - measuring cups and spoons
  - tape measures, hourglasses, and other measuring tools
  - old clocks and watches

- Encourage children to use counting and numbers for specific purposes. When counting and numbers are necessary, children have a meaningful way to practice counting and to use numbers. For example, children may need to count
    - the number of children who can work in the woodworking area at a given time.
    - the number of teaspoons, tablespoons, or cups required to make pudding, bread, or other foods using one-cup cooking. Barbara Johnson-Foote (2001) has developed cooking experiences in which each child follows a recipe for making just one portion of gingerbread, lemonade, and other healthful foods. By doing so, each child is following the pictures and printed recipe, measuring individual portions of food, to make his or her own serving.
- Just for fun, ask children to find out
    - how many children in the group are wearing something red, something blue, something old and something new
    - the number of children wearing red shoes, blue shoes, new shoes, buckle shoes, or tie shoes
    - how many children have a cat for a pet, a dog, a fish, or no pet at all
    - the number of children who like a particular color, poem, story, movie, or food
    - how many children have baby brothers or sisters, how many have older brothers and sisters, and how many have no brothers and sisters
    - the number of birds that come to a feeder in a given amount of time
    - the number of flowers that are in bloom on the scarlet runner bean vines the children planted

◆ Not everything children count has to be totally concrete. For example, they could count
    - the number of days until someone's birthday. To make the task more concrete, make a paper chain with the number of days children have to wait for a birthday, a field trip, a party, or other special event. Each day, have a child take off one of the paper rings. The number remaining is the same as the number of days children have to wait for the event.
    - how old a child is on his or her birthday. They could count fingers, chips, blocks, candles, and so on to make the task concrete.
    - the number of different games, songs, or poems they know.

2. Children Will Learn the Names of the Numerals and to Write Them

Because of the structure of the English language, children in the United States learn number names, at least through the teens, essentially by rote. Children often use idiosyncratic number names showing that they do not yet understand the base 10 underlying larger number names (NRC, 2001).

Even though learning the conventional names of numbers involves rote memory, knowledge of number names and conceptual understanding of number go hand in hand. Further, the more embedded children's learning is in meaningful experiences, the greater the conceptual learning.

- Use children's literature to enhance children's knowledge of the names of numerals. There are thousands of counting books available. *Ten Little Ladybugs* (Gerth, 2001), *Anno's Magic Seeds* (Anno, 1999), *Ten Little Rabbits* (Grossman, 1999), and *Fish Eyes: A Book You Can Count On* (Ehlert, 2001) are examples of excellent counting books. To use the books effectively
    - hold individual toddlers on your lap and read a counting book together. Point to the numerals as you name them. Three-year-olds will enjoy listening over and over again to Jack Wood's *Moo, Moo, Brown Cow* (1992).
    - obtain big books to read to the entire class, using a pointer or running your hands under the words and numerals as you read.
    - have flannel, Velcro, or magnetic numerals, and hold them up as they appear in a story. Place them on a board or hand them out to the children, who will hold them up when they appear again in the story or when you reread the story.

- Follow up story reading with a related activity. For example, after reading *Fish Eyes: A Book You Can Count On* (Ehlert, 2001), you could count the number of eyes of each fish in the aquarium and the number of eyes each child has, and then find living creatures without eyes—starfish, jellyfish, mollusks, and so on. Go on to count how many legs spiders and insects have.

    After reading *Anno's Magic Seeds* (Anno, 1999), each child could plant their own seeds. Label the plots with children's names. Count how long it takes for each seed to sprout, how tall each sprout grows, and how many days it takes for blossoms and then fruit or vegetables to grow. Scarlet runner beans are good to plant because they sprout and grow rapidly, helping to hold young children's attention.

    Read Ezra Jack Keats' *Over in the Meadow* (1990), and teach children to sing the song. Divide the group up to take on the roles of birds, toads, and so on. When it's time for the birds to say "We sing, said the three," the children acting as birds, or whatever animal, sing out the phrase.

- Make your own number book stories. Make books of newsprint pages with construction paper covers.
    - Give 3-year-olds a book of three to five newsprint pages. Stamp the numeral 1 on the first page, 2 on the second page, and so on. Children can use rubber stamps of different objects and things, attach stickers, or draw the number of objects.
    - Four-year-olds can be given books with 10 numerals, and choose to use stickers, print with rubber stamps, use other collage materials, or draw pictures of the number of objects that belong on each page. Five-year-olds can also choose to write the numerals.

        Remember that the objects children choose to print, stick, or draw on their pages do not have to be all the same. A set can consist of different objects. For example, a child could illustrate the page with the numeral 3 by choosing to place stickers of a car, a duck, and a flower on the page.

- Make flannel board cutouts of numerals, or use any type of plastic or wooden numerals, for children to take turns placing on a flannel board or standing and holding up as the numerals appear in a chant.
- Use numerals in directions for open snack. Some centers have open snack, with children serving themselves. To make open snack efficient, teachers use a display stand with simple directions. Make sure children wash their hands prior to making snacks. As a safety precaution, each child would be provided with their own set of utensils, and adult guidance would stop children from sticking either fingers or knives they've just licked back into the peanut butter or jelly.

◆ Provide children with many opportunities that encourage them to write numerals as well as letters.

- In the writing center include plastic numerals as well as letters. Also have a set of rubber stamp numerals, sets of other rubber stamps, and markers and papers for children to use to practice printing or writing numerals. Or children can use computers to keyboard numerals, name these, and then write them.
- Provide calendars that have space for writing. Put these in the writing center or housekeeping area along with markers. You don't need to provide any directions; children will use them in different ways. Most, however, will begin copying the numeral in the space, giving them needed practice in writing numerals.
- Place a number of small chalkboards and chalk on a table along with wooden or plastic numerals. Again, no directions are necessary. Children will draw, scribble, and write on the boards, but with the numerals as a prompt, they will incorporate numerals in their writing.
- Give children flexible wire or pipe cleaners to make numerals. Or children could make numerals from Play Doh, clay, or other modeling material.
- In the writing center, children could choose how they want to make numerals. They could pick plastic or wooden numerals from a box and name them, print the numerals with rubber printing stamps, use a computer to print numerals, or use paper and markers to write them.

3. Children Will Learn to Count Sequentially

◆ Chant many counting rhymes until children know them by heart.

For some counting rhymes, children can pretend to be the characters. For instance, when you chant "Five Little Speckled Frogs," invite one child to be a frog. To avoid conflict, designate a "pool" ahead of time: "When it's your turn to jump into the pool, where will you jump?" Children may choose a place on the floor, or decide to jump back to where they were sitting.

The first child will select enough children, counting herself, to make five frogs. Children mimic eating the lunch, then jump into the "pool" when the chant tells them to. When that group is finished, ask another child to start the game again until all who want to play have a turn at being a frog.

It's important for children to do the choosing. Yes, it puts them in control, which is important, but it also gives them the opportunity to count themselves and figure out how many more children they need to make five frogs. If working with 5-year-olds, extend the number of frogs to 10.

Do the same for other counting rhymes:

"Five Little (or Ten) Little Chickadees"

"Five (or Ten) Little Pumpkins"

"Ten in a Bed"

"Five Little Monkeys"

4. Children Will Have Meaningful Opportunities to Count Using One-to-one Correspondence.

You will want children to pair real objects and at the same time count the objects to find out what the number is. Begin with natural situations, where there is a need for matching (NCTM, 1975).

◆ Dressing activities are a natural. While children are dressing, you might say the following:

"Look, you have two hands and two mittens. Put one on each hand. How many hands do you have? How many mittens?"

"Put one arm in this sleeve, the other in this sleeve. How many arms do you have? How many sleeves?"

"How many feet do you have? Put a sock on each foot. How many socks do you have?"

"There's a button for each hole. How many buttons are there? Let's count. How many holes are there?"

◆ Everyday activities offer situations for matching one object or item to another.

- During snacks and lunchtimes, give children the opportunity to place one napkin, fork, spoon, and glass at each place. Each child chooses one piece of fruit, one cracker, or one piece of cheese.

- Have fieldwork offer other matching opportunities. Each child finds another child to work with. Each child in a team takes a a science kit to work with. (A science kit—an old backpack—contains a magnifying glass, a tape measure, pads or paper and markers, tweezers, and other science tools.)

- To complete an art project, give each child one pair of scissors, a glue stick, and paper.

- Play musical chairs with enough chairs for all the children. Make the point that there is a chair for each child when the music stops.

- During music time, have children clap their hands once to each beat of a drum, clap once for each syllable in their name, or clap when they sing or hear rhyming words.

- Construct matching games for children to play with and manipulate.

- Glue buttons of different sizes, shapes, and colors on a piece of cardboard or plywood. Give children a box of assorted buttons (all too large to fit in noses, mouths, ears, or other places) and ask them to give each of the buttons on the board a partner button. Children do not need to match buttons by color, size, or so on, only to give each one a partner button.

- Play with parquet blocks. Place a row of blocks in front of a child and ask him or her to give each block a partner.
- Make "match me" cards. Make two sets of cards with stickers in different arrangements for each number from 1 to 10. Children are to find all the cards that represent a numeral, for example, all the cards that have 4 stickers, or 6, or 10. Children match the number of stickers visually or by counting.

5. Children Will Begin to Use Number Operations in Connection with Their Daily Activities

Preschool children have been observed using a variety of strategies that involve number operations. Most are able to use counting to perform simple addition and subtraction involving a single item by at least 3 years of age (NRC, 2001). The variety of strategies—adding on, using fingers or items to count—leads researchers to conclude that children invent their own ways of adding and subtracting.

The role of teachers, then, is to observe children as they work with numbers, and try to understand what children are thinking. To better understand their thinking, you might ask children how they found the right number of items or why they did what they did. Then, based on children's existing knowledge, teachers plan new experiences that clarify, expand, or extend that existing knowledge.

◆ Everyday problems need number operations to be solved. You might

- ask children to count how many more children can work at the woodworking center at a given time.
- have children count the number of chairs that need to be added to a group of chairs so each child has a place to sit. Or have children count the number of chairs that need to be removed to match the size of the group.
- involve children in using addition or subtraction in connection with their routines. For example, choose one child to pick enough children to make six children to take their turn brushing their teeth or getting their coats from the cubbies.
- let children count the number of children who want to be in a center, who want to play a game, or who want to use a new piece of equipment. Then have them count the number who will have to wait for their turn.

◆ Use games that involve taking away and adding. Playing the following games involves individual children or groups in counting, developing their disposition to use numbers and counting. The teacher might suggest a game to be played and demonstrate the game with a small group of children, or children could select a game from the counting table or math area (Seefeldt & Barbour, 1998).

- Mystery Box

Prepare a number of boxes by cutting a hole in one side of each box and placing a given number of small objects in each box. The child reaches into a box, feels the objects, counts them, and tells how many objects are in the box. Take the objects out of the box and count them again. Begin by placing two or three objects in a box, and increase the numbers of objects as children gain counting skills.

Experience 1 ◆ Young Children Develop Ideas of Number and Counting

- Bowling

  The child rolls a ball to knock down a group of objects—empty, cleaned milk cartons; empty squirt bottles; or juice cans. After children roll the ball, they count the number of objects they've knocked down and begin again. The goal is to knock all of the objects down. The game can be played alone, with a friend or two, or with the teacher, who will record children's knowledge of counting.

- Collections

  You'll need boxes and a collection of objects that fit in the boxes. Empty boxes are labeled "1," "2," "3," and so on. The child selects the specified number of objects from those provided to match the numeral on a box and puts them in the box. The game can be taken outside, and children can fill the boxes with found objects, rocks, stones, pinecones, or leaves. The idea is to count, so the objects in the box, or set, do not have to be all alike.

- Dominoes

  Demonstrate to a child or a small group of children how to play dominoes, matching a domino with four spots with another that has an equal number of spots.

- Calendar Bingo

  Mount pages from old or unused calendars on heavy cardboard. Identical mounted calendar pages are cut into individual number cards. The children match the individual numerals by placing them on the corresponding numerals on the uncut calendar.

- Button, Button

  Working with one child or a small group of children, give each child a handful of buttons of the same size, color, and shape. Allow children time to play with the buttons, trade them, match them, or make patterns with them, and then give children directions to follow: "Move two buttons to the middle of the table," "Put three buttons on top of one another," "Give four buttons to the person next to you." The number of buttons, and what children are to do with them, increases in difficulty as children mature and gain number concepts.

◇ **Reflecting**

Children can reflect on their counting experiences by organizing, presenting, applying, and communicating their knowledge of number and counting.

- Make number charts for the room as a way for children to organize their ideas of number and counting. Print the numbers and number names on sheets of large construction paper. Have children make sets of small pictures or stickers to place on the charts.

- Structure opportunities for children to apply numbers during the day. Ask them to count the number of children, apples, markers, or other objects needed. Ask them how many they have, and how many more items they'll need.

- Make certain that children represent their experiences in drawings, paintings, or other creative ways. By doing so, they must call up mental memories—ideas of number—find a way to transfer these to paper, and think of how they can do so.

• From time to time ask children to demonstrate their counting skills to others. They might "read" a counting book to a group of younger or older children. Or they could take home a counting book to "read" to their parents.

◇ Extending and Expanding to the Primary Grades

• Five-year-olds or older children can make fold-over booklets. Fold a piece of 12" × 18" construction paper in half and then in thirds. Cut between the folds to make doors. On the cover they print the numeral and inside draw a picture of one, two, three, and so on objects. Children over age 6 can write a story as well.

• Create a mural depicting a chant for 5-year-olds. For instance, if children love *Ten Little Rabbits* (Grossman, 1999), you could take a long strip of mural paper and vertically mark spaces for the ten numerals.

Children working as small groups or individuals can volunteer to illustrate the numerals, drawing or painting the required number of rabbits for each space. Have children choose which numeral they'll work on so each child gets a turn and no child has to draw 10 rabbits by him- or herself. For younger children, choose a less complex chant and perhaps use only three or five numerals at a time.

◇ Documenting Children's Learning

This web illustrates the mathematical concepts inherent in learning numbers and counting. It illustrates, as well, content from other areas of the curriculum that is integrated into counting experiences.

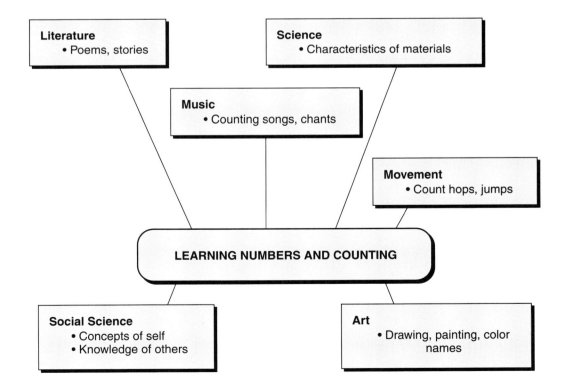

Tear-Out Sheet 1

Date:

Dear Parents:

We will be teaching children to count and use numbers through the daily activities in the classroom. You can do the same at home. While you're sorting laundry, setting the table, and shopping at the supermarket, remember to use numbers as you talk with your children about what you are doing. For example, you might

- ask your child to help you pick out three pennies from your purse so you'll have change for the cashier. Or you might give children a dollar bill, or enough change to equal a dollar, to take to the dollar store and buy any item they wish.
- count the change you receive from cashiers in front of the children.
- count the corners of the bed as your children help you finish making it.
- have children help you set the table, placing one fork, spoon, napkin, glass, and so on at each placemat.
- while dressing children, count toes, noses, buttonholes, shoes, socks, fingers, and mittens.
- count the number of children to invite to a party.
- count the number of teddy bears in the child's room.
- count the number of hugs and kisses you give to each of your children before bedtime.

Probably you've been counting and using number with your children for a long time. If you have a few moments, share your ideas with us. You can call or e-mail at _____, or just tell us your ideas when we see you. We'll make a list of these to send to each child's family.

We enjoy working with you and your children.

Our best,

Date:

Dear Families:

    We wanted you to know how much your children enjoyed working with a set of parquet blocks we brought out this week. The children used the blocks to sort, make patterns, and count. If you have small items at home, you can continue your children's counting experiences.

    When we first put out the parquet blocks, we gave children plenty of time to just move them around, exploring what they were and what could be done with them. When children tired of just playing around, one of the teachers sat at the table with the children.

    She started by making a pattern of blocks. She stacked two square blocks together, followed by a triangle block, then two more square blocks, and so on. She asked children to make a pattern just like hers. When they caught on to making patterns, counting as they did so, she asked children to take turns being the leader and making a pattern for the others to follow.

    Another day a different teacher sat with children and the parquet blocks. After children had experimented with them, she began to make sets of blocks. She selected two square blocks and a round block, asking how many were in her "set," then asking children to make a set that had one more block than she had. Children then took the lead, making sets and asking other children to add two, three, and more blocks to their sets, or to make sets with one, two, and three blocks less than were in their set.

    The next day baskets were added to the parquet blocks, and children counted round, triangle, and square blocks into their baskets, finding out who had the most blocks.

    Feel free to borrow a set of parquet blocks. They're on the lending table; just sign out for them. Or you and your children could play similar games with a deck of cards, any kind of plastic or wooden chips you have, coins, large buttons, bottle caps, and any other small objects.

    We hope you and your children have as much fun as we did exploring the parquet blocks, and learn as much as well.

Our best,

Tear-Out Sheet 3

Date:

Dear Families:

We are attaching a copy of the finger plays and counting songs your children enjoy when they're at the center. If you read or chant these to your children, you'll find that they have memorized most of the chants, and can count sequentially.

Enjoy,

Date:

Dear Parents:

Want to learn how your children build mathematic concepts? Come to our math workshop on _____ at _____. We will demonstrate how children learn math concepts by playing with blocks and other small manipulatives. You will learn several games to play with your children to reinforce their ideas about mathematics.

Call or e-mail us at _____ to let us know if you will be coming to the math workshop.

Sincerely,

Experience 2

Young Children Learn the Basic Concepts of Algebra

FOR THE TEACHER

◇ What You'll Need to Know

Teachers of young children often feel insecure about conveying math concepts to their students since they themselves often had poor experiences when they were in school. Then, too, they may not have had the formative math experiences in their early years that would lead them to view math as problem solving, communicating with others, using reasoning skills, and drawing connections. When problem solving is viewed as key to mathematics learning, it becomes obvious to teachers that young children are ready to learn math. They are natural problem solvers who are curious about everything in their environment and ask questions that invite the investigation of answers.

When told that children in prekindergarten through grade 2 are expected to meet certain standards in the content area of algebra, teachers may well ask themselves if they are providing the foundation for the important abstract concepts of algebra to come in the later school years. Perhaps it is helpful to view algebra as the sum of various activities that young children already do spontaneously, but will need lots of opportunities to try in many situations and with diverse strategies. Basic experiences with algebra involve

- the skills of classifying, sorting, and ordering objects
- the understanding of patterns in all aspects of their existence such as color, shape, number, and texture as well as those involving kinesthetic, tactile, visual, or auditory stimuli
- the use of concrete and pictorial representations that will later develop into symbolic notations
- the addition and subtraction of "things," pictures, and symbols
- the understanding of quantitative changes in things such as plants growing larger
- the understanding of qualitative changes in things such as that one tree is larger than the one next to it

The teacher will want to provide many experiences for young children that foster these skills. Some will come as incidental learnings while others will be carefully planned to illustrate a basic concept. Gradually, through active experiences with the components of algebra, children will form the foundations on which later abstract learning can be built.

Copley (2000) suggests that there are questions specific to patterns, functions, and algebra. They are designed to facilitate children's thinking and sharpen their problem-solving skills. Examples are

Do you see a pattern? Tell me about it.

Can you feel a pattern on that piece of carpet? Tell me about it.

What comes next? How could we make this pattern with these different materials?

How can we remember this pattern? How can we make a picture that will help us? Could we use numbers instead?

Can you dance your pattern?

Can you clap your pattern?

◇ Key Concepts

- Patterns exist everywhere in a variety of shapes, sizes, colors, numbers, and textures.
- It is possible to repeat and extend patterns as in music.
- Groups of various items may be sorted, classified, and ordered by many attributes.
- The addition and subtraction of whole numbers may be represented using objects, pictures, and symbols.
- Addition and subtraction sentences may be constructed. "More" suggests addition, and "less" suggests subtraction.
- A variety of things may change in quality and in quantity.

◇ Goals and Objectives

The following depend on age/grade:

Children will identify patterns in a variety of ways, not only in numbers, but also in designs, music, and movement.

Children will create and interpret patterns.

Children will repeat and extend patterns.

Children will describe quantitative and qualitative changes in living things. This goal is best left for kindergarten or early elementary children.

Children will be introduced to symbols through concrete representations.

Children will sort, classify, and order a variety of concrete objects by various attributes.

Children will begin to use simple mathematical terminology.

◇ What You'll Need

The National Council of Teachers of Mathematics (see references) has many fine publications and Web resources. Unfortunately, the authors of this book have found that few of them are helpful to teachers of preschool-aged children. The joint position statement of NAEYC and NCTM (April, 2002) suggests that algebraic thinking should receive somewhat less emphasis in the early childhood curriculum with the exception of patterning, which merits special mention because it is accessible and interesting to young children, eventually undergirds all algebraic thinking, and supports the development of other conceptual areas. Young children also sort and classify spontaneously and can be helped to understand and reflect upon what they are doing.

Keeping in mind that children construct their own knowledge through active experiences, the following books will help you to refresh your memory on algebra and to plan activities for the children you teach:

Mathematics for the young child. Edited by Joseph N. Payne. (1990). National Council of Teachers of Mathematics. This book is designed for teacher educators and teachers of children in preschool through grade 4. It is full of activities; however, a close examination shows fewer for the younger grades. Some activities can be adapted for younger children.

Children search for patterns and relationships.

Wonderful world of mathematics: A critically annotated list of children's books in mathematics, 2nd ed. By Diane Thiessen, Margaret Matthias, and Jacquelin Smith. (1998). National Council of Teachers of Mathematics. A valuable collection of short reviews of children's books with mathematical content. Again you may want to look closely for books for preschoolers. If you do, you will be rewarded with an excellent book to inspire an active mathematics experience.

Count on math: Activities for small hands and lively minds. By Pam Schiller and Lynne Peterson. (1997). Gryphon House, Inc. An activity-oriented program for children ages 3 to 7.

Math arts: Exploring math through art for 3 to 6 year olds. By Mary Ann Kohl and Cindy Gainer. (1997). Gryphon House. Many good ideas for using art to foster emergent math skills and concepts.

Navigating through algebra in prekindergarten–grade 2 (with CD-ROM). By Carol Greenes, Mary Cavanagh, Linda Dacey, Carol Findell, and Marian Small. (2001). National Council of Teachers of Mathematics. Demonstrates how some fundamental concepts of algebra can be introduced. The most helpful part for teachers of young children may be the section on repeating and growing patterns.

Picturing math. By Carol Otis Hurst and Rebecca Otis. (1996). SRA/McGraw-Hill. Has an excellent chapter on patterns and picture books. Hurst and Otis include the developmental stages in introducing patterns, a few pattern activities for several age groups, and annotated picture books for patterns.

Children's Books

Aardema, V. (1975). *Why mosquitoes buzz in people's ears.* New York: Dial Books for Young Readers.

Anno, M. (translation and special contents of this book copyright in 1987 by Philomel Books, a division of Putnam & Grosset Group). *Anno's math games.*

Brown, M. W. (1947). *Goodnight moon/Buenas noches luna.* New York: Harper & Row.

Dee, R. (1988). *Two ways to count to ten: A Liberian folktale* (retold by Ruby Dee). New York: Henry Holt.

De Regniers, B. S. (1985). *So many cats!* Wilmington, MA: Houghton Mifflin.

Fox, M. (1990). *Shoes from Grandpa.* London: A Division of Watts Publishing Group.

Hoban, T. (1986). *Shapes, shapes, shapes.* New York: Greenwillow Books.

Hoban, T. (1987). *Dots, spots, speckles, and stripes.* New York: Greenwillow.

Hutchins, P. (1986). *The doorbell rang.* New York: Mulberry Books.

Martin, B., Jr., & Archambault, J. (1989). *Chicka chicka boom boom.* New York: Simon & Schuster Books for Young Readers.

Marvelous math: A book of poems. (1997). Selected by L. B. Hopkins. New York: Simon and Schuster Books for Young Readers.

McMillan, B. (1986). *Becca backward, Becca, forward: A book of concept pairs.* New York: HarperCollins.

Reid, M. (1990). *The button box.* New York: Dutton.

Other Things You'll Need

- Containers of all types for sorting including egg cartons, plastic sewing boxes, and toolboxes
- Magnetic boards and magnetic pieces
- Objects of all kinds for sorting, classifying, and ordering. These may vary depending on whether the activities are conducted indoors or outdoors.
- Numeral cards
- Cubes and pattern blocks
- Beads and other materials to string
- Pegs and pegboards
- Flannel boards with flannel pieces to manipulate
- Geoboards
- Parquetry blocks and patterns
- Colored tiles
- Balances and weights
- Music that has rhythm and repetition
- Paper, drawing tools, collage materials, wallpaper, sponges, paints, and other art supplies
- School calendar
- Magazines and photographs featuring patterns on buildings, sidewalks, and so forth
- Access to the outdoor environment to identify patterns in nature

◇ The Home-School Connection

There are many things that parents can do to enhance emergent math skills and concepts in algebra without altering the daily routine or buying expensive materials and equipment. There are plenty of things in the home, yard, grocery store, and so on to provide curious children with active experiences in math.

The U.S. Department of Education has published a book for parents and their young children, *Early Childhood: Where Learning Begins—Mathematics: Mathematical Activities for Parents and Their 2- to 5-Year-Old Children,* (June 1999). It may be obtained from the U.S. Department of Education or from the Web. It emphasizes problem solving, communication, and questioning skills for both children and parents. The following daily activities are suggested for enhancing emergent skills in algebra. You can convey them to parents through a newsletter, a bulletin board, a conference, or an algebra party.

When children get dressed, ask them to look for patterns in their clothing. Then ask them to describe the patterns. Discuss the events of the day with your children. This will help them to understand that the sequence of events is another pattern. Setting the table at mealtime also emphasizes patterns. The knife and fork are always put in the same place relative to each other.

On the way to school, point out how the shapes of street signs help people know what each sign means. The link between symbols and the concepts they represent is key to algebra learning, but not always clear to young children. Children will eventually make the connection.

When waiting in the doctor's office or other places, encourage children to look for patterns on the rug, wallpaper, or furniture. At the grocery store, younger children can understand that the managers of the store have sorted items by type and placed them together in aisles. For older children, point out that each aisle has a number. Let your children help you find an aisle by its number or find in which aisle a particular item is located. When you get home, let your children sort the groceries into piles or however you want them put away. Any time the family laundry is done is a chance for sorting and matching games. Children learn the concept of multiple ways to sort and re-sort.

◇ Evaluating and Assessing Children's Learning

Teachers have a responsibility to assess their own teaching effectiveness as well as children's learning and development of emergent concepts in algebra. Assessment will be a continuous activity done on an individual and group basis using

- observations
- small and large group discussions with students as they work individually and in groups
- structured interviews with students at intervals during the school year
- children's math journals
- portfolios of children's work
- children's self-evaluations and dictated stories about math concepts

The tear-out sheets on pages 83–84 at the end of this experience can be used at different times during the school year to chart growth in children's thinking, and to help you plan your curriculum on the basis of children's current understandings.

FOR THE CHILDREN

This section attempts to treat each of the components of early numeracy in algebra. First, the search for patterns and relationships will be discussed. Then, the chapter will treat sorting, classifying, and ordering. Finally, ideas for the addition and subtraction of whole numbers using objects, pictures, and symbols will be presented. The teacher will recognize that each of the components is connected and know to examine each experience for all possible facets of concept development. The teacher will want to encourage children to keep a math journal to record the concepts they have learned. For younger children, this might consist of simple labeled drawings, or an illustration of a basic concept such as the pattern on a leaf. Older children may make drawings of their investigations of objects and symbols and provide an explanation for what they did.

1. The Search for Patterns and Relationships

Richardson and Salkeld (1995) see the search for patterns as the search for an underlying structure in whatever situation we find ourselves. Patterns can be experienced in a variety of ways, not only in numbers but also in designs and arrangements, and in recurring events, such the flow of the day or the days of the week. The order and structure that is present in our number system is revealed when we begin looking for patterns. Children need to use their understanding of patterns as a tool for solving problems and making predictions. Take every opportunity to have children look for patterns inside and outside the classroom. Their clothes, the rug, and the classroom itself form a pattern. Outside, children may collect leaves and discover the different patterns in each.

Researchers suggest that there are developmental stages in the understanding of patterns. Prekindergarten students are ready for an introduction to the idea of patterns and simple examples of patterns. They already recognize many patterns in their lives, such as those in daily routines (see "The Home-School Connection").

In kindergarten, students can find patterns in a wide variety of contexts. They can describe patterns to each other, extend patterns, and represent patterns using manipulatives.

By first and second grade, the ability to recognize complex patterns increases, and children get better at creating their own patterns. Later they can manipulate those patterns in variety of ways.

GENERALIZATIONS ABOUT NATURAL AND MAN-MADE PATTERNS

- Patterns are made of parts.
- Patterns have defining characteristics.
- Patterns are repetitious.
- Patterns provide order.
- Patterns can be used to predict outcomes.
- Patterns provide a framework for learning.
- Patterns can be simple or complex.
- Patterns can overlay one another.
- Patterns are everywhere.
- Patterns can change.

Start with simple activities for younger children and do not ask them for a "right answer." Their experimentation and observation skills will lead them to mature conclusions as they progress.

- ◆ Read and chant *Chicka Chicka Boom Boom* by Bill Martin and John Archambault. Ask young children to predict what comes next. The pattern is in the rhythmic chant and in the alphabetical order of the letters as they climb the tree. A few children may recognize the order of the alphabet. For younger children, play "head, shoulders, knees, and toes" to become familiar with patterns. Later extend this pattern to "clap, shoulders, shoulders, knees; clap, shoulders, shoulders, knees." Ask children how they would describe this pattern with ABCs or symbols. Many children will catch on that the pattern is "ABBC." Some children may be ready to generalize the "ABBC" pattern to colored tiles or other manipulatives, another symbolic representation.

- ◆ Use art activities to encourage children's recognition and creation of patterns. Using watercolors and wet sponges of various shapes, encourage children to create patterns on paper. Ask them how they could repeat the pattern by adding more shapes. Be careful to encourage them to look closely at the pattern they have just created. Also ask them what would happen if you added shapes (in a predictable way). Then the pattern would grow.

    Have children create collages using tissue paper and old magazines with interesting patterns. Have them describe the patterns they have created. Ask them if they can glue or paste pieces of wallpaper to construction paper and keep the pattern. Encourage the children to discuss their art with each other, identifying similarities and differences.

- ◆ Use the school calendar to help children identify a visual pattern, but also patterns that occur in everyday life. Ask children to fill in days of the week or important dates with certain colors. Point out how the calendar is a thing (symbol) that represents the days in weeks, months, and years.

- ◆ Use books of photographs and other children's books to illustrate patterns. *Goodnight Moon* by Margaret Wise Brown is full of patterns. Colors darken as night approaches, and toys change in size. The author has carefully based her book on the patterns of going to sleep. *Dots, Spots, Speckles, and Stripes* by Tana Hoban uses vivid photographs to illustrate patterns in feathers, flowers, people, and animals.

- ◆ Use popular physical activities to illustrate the concept of pattern: for example, step, hop, hop, step, hop, hop; or hands up, hands down, hands out. Once the children have mastered a pattern, they will be able to predict the movement that comes next. Always ask them to describe the pattern. Older children may be able to explain it in symbols.

- ◆ Use music to illustrate the concept of pattern. Try "Jambo and Other Call-and-Response Songs and Chants" by Ella Jenkins, Smithsonian Folkways, 45017; "You'll Sing a Song and I'll Sing a Song" by Ella Jenkins, SfW, 45010; and "Let's Build a Rhythm—This Is Rhythm" by Ella Jenkins, SfW, 45028. These discs should assist children in building concepts of pattern through music.

- ◆ Have children use their tactile sense to build the concept of pattern. Provide them with raised patterns to feel or a piece of carpet with a pattern.

2. Sorting, Classifying, and Ordering Objects by Size, Number, and Other Properties

Seefeldt and Barbour (1998) suggest that before children can classify, they must have some concept of "belongingness," "put together," and "alike." Consequently, the role of the teacher is to provide children with many experiences with the manipulation of materials.

- ◆ Provide children with boxes of scrap materials: velvet squares, tweeds, and net—all cut into uniform sizes and shapes for feeling, sorting, and classifying according to texture. Once they have performed the operation according to texture, ask that they try to use another attribute such as color. Using other categories of things will keep the interest of the children alive. Try

   bells of all types—this adds the attribute of sound

   greeting cards

   a button box

   shells, seeds, leaves, and rocks found in the outdoor environment

   bolts, nails, screws—this adds the dimension of function

- ◆ Provide children with yarn, sticks, uniform blocks, and shapes to order as to size, color, and so on. The older the children, the more ways they will find to order a set of objects.

3. Addition and Subtraction of Whole Numbers, Using Objects, Pictures and Symbols

   Children will need to have a background in observing objects and pictures that "stand for" something to build an understanding of the use of symbols in mathematics. For example, when on a walking field trip, point out the stop sign. Ask children what it stands for. Yes, it stands for the action "stop." If you have signs in your block building area, be sure to show children how the symbols stand for something. Addition and subtraction also involve the understanding of words such as "more" and "less," as well as counting skills.

   - ◆ Read the children *Two Ways to Count to Ten: A Liberian Folktale* by Ruby Dee. The book illustrates two ways to count to ten—by twos as well as ones. Take various even numbers and see if the children can figure out ways to count to the end number. If the children are young, give them any number of manipulatives and see if they can sort them into equal groups that will add up to the original number given them. The folktale also illustrates the point that the winner is the one who thinks carefully about how he will solve the problem.

   - ◆ Read the children *The Doorbell Rang* by Pat Hutchins. Ma bakes cookies for Sam and Victoria to share. But—the doorbell rings and each time it rings, more and more friends come to share the plate of cookies. This leaves fewer and fewer cookies for the children to divide until Grandma arrives with fresh cookies. Divide the class into pairs. Give each pair 20 identical objects and ask them to find various ways to put them into equal groups. Record their findings. Then have them repeat the activity two more times, first using 18 objects and then using 12 objects. Take 12 students at a time. Ask them to place themselves into two equal groups, then three equal groups, and finally four equal groups. Bake cookies with your class and follow the steps in the book, making sure that the cookies are divided equally.

◇ Reflecting

Ask children to organize their experiences. Provide them with exhibit space so that they can display their sponge paintings and collage patterned art. Kindergartners may want to have a table of classifications based on different attributes. The teacher should encourage them to carefully label the concept they wish to convey. Also make sure that children's math journals are up-to-date, illustrated, and, if appropriate, displayed next to their experiments.

Have a party! Invite family members and the school community to a pattern party. Exhibit various patterns on the bulletin board and throughout the room. Have children create some simple games involving objects for younger siblings to sort and tricky patterns for parents and other older family members to identify. Cook food with shapes and in various sizes such as pasta and cookies made with cookie cutters. Serve the food to guests at your mathematics party. Play "patterned" music, or perform movement exercises. Have the children sing songs that rhyme, repeat, or have numbers in them. See if they can teach them to their families. Ella Jenkins and Hap Palmer have many tapes and CDs of interactive patterned songs. Display children's books about mathematics for parents to examine. (See the tear-out sheet on page 82.)

◇ Extending and Expanding to the Primary Grades

Children in the early primary grades can do the following:

- Understand the concepts of repeating and growing patterns, and articulate the principles behind them. The teacher may start by giving them the principle (add two cubes to each side) and then let them experiment with different ideas.

- Understand more complex patterns and how they are used. A famous illustrator of children's picture books, Jerry Pinkney, uses quilts in each of his books. He believes they are the fiber that holds a culture together. (See *Mirandy and Brother Wind* by Patricia C. McKissack, illustrated by Jerry Pinkney, New York: Alfred A. Knopf.) The teacher may ask older children to discuss the concept of pattern in this or other contexts. How would we function without patterns? Read the poem "Math Makes Me Feel Safe" by Betsy Franco in *Marvelous Math: A Book of Poems*. (1997), selected by L. B. Hopkins.

- Utilize more abstract concepts in ordering or determining what is different in a pattern. *Anno's Math Games* has many challenges for the young elementary school student in the area of emergent algebra skills. The games are also appropriate for other math content areas.

- Understand simple equations, especially in concrete form. For example, using balance scales and Unifix cubes, children can experiment with balancing sets of concrete objects. Teachers may extend this knowledge to exploring various ways of representing their equations in conventional ways. Experimentation leads to making predictions of what will happen.

- Understand that items can be multiply classified. Read *The Button Box* by M. Reid (1990). In this book, a young boy explores his grandmother's box of buttons, grouping or classifying them according to various qualities. He imagines interesting stories behind the different buttons. Examples of classifications for the same group of buttons can be color, smallest to largest, and then largest to smallest (reversibility). Then ask children to dictate or write a story about their buttons or create pictures according to the color of the buttons they have.

- Gain familiarity with symbols and be encouraged to create their own signs to represent actions, such as "stop," and "go," and "slow." These can be used around the classroom.

- More easily describe qualitative and quantitative changes. Linking mathematics with science investigations may facilitate the acquisition of these concepts. Describing the changes in plants and seeds and using comparison words help children to understand change. Measuring and recording changes in height or weight in journals or on graphs helps with quantitative thinking and connects to concepts of data collection and interpretation.

- Ask better and more specific questions and make better predictions.

- Design their own simple experiments and math games.

- Utilize computers to locate the Web sites for mathematics resources. Teachers will want to make sure that the sites are suitable.

- Build a larger vocabulary of mathematical terms. These may be recorded in their math journals, put on word walls, and posted in the math area of the classroom for easy reference.

◇ Documenting Children's Learning

Under the section on reflecting, many ideas are presented for documenting children's learning. Both teachers and children should take part. A web can document the concepts, learnings, skills, and attitudes that children develop through their active experiences with emergent concepts of algebra. The web may hang in the classroom as a reminder of the integrated learning that took place. Teacher checksheets, word walls, teacher/child discussions, and portfolios of children's work provide authentic assessments of children's achievement.

Tear-Out Sheet 1

Date:

Dear Parents:

As part of our mathematics curriculum for this year, we are working on the theme, The Search for Patterns and Relationships. We will start with looking for patterns inside and outside the classroom. Then we will plan various art, music, and movement activities to reinforce the concept. There are many things that you can do to help us at school and at home. We would love to have you come in and volunteer whenever you can. Please let us know a bit ahead so we will be prepared for your visit. But if you can't fit a visit into school hours, please help us teach your children about patterns at home.

When you go out, ask your children to observe what patterns they see in the natural world or on buildings. Let them tell you about it. You might also want to sing simple songs with patterns or clap out patterns. We will send you some samples in the backpack to come.

When children ask questions, sometimes it is easier to ignore them or answer with a word or two. Posing questions is really what mathematics is about, so we would really like it if you could take the time to answer your children's questions. You don't have to be a mathematician. Sometimes children will think more if you respond with a question: "What do you think?" We have a number of good fiction and nonfiction books that relate to patterns in math to lend, so let us know if you would like to borrow one.

Your children will be keeping a math journal. Encourage them to illustrate their observations about patterns, and perhaps they can dictate sentences to you about natural or man-made patterns.

Thank you for helping us with our new math unit. Your children are building the skills that they will need for the study of mathematics in the later school years.

Sincerely,

Permission is granted by the publisher to reproduce this page.

Tear-Out Sheet 2

Date:

Dear Parents:

In the next few days, we will be sending a small backpack home with your children with suggestions for things that they can do at home to expand their mathematics concepts. The experiences should be fun for everyone. They include things like singing songs, making patterns with scrap materials, and keeping a home calendar of evening activities and things you do on weekends.

Each kit will contain simple directions. Don't worry if the projects aren't perfect. Children learn from their mistakes too.

In each kit, you will find a cassette of songs by Ella Jenkins. Each song illustrates how patterns work in music. Perhaps you and your child would like to sing a song and teach it to the class at the upcoming class math party. Let us know which one you pick so that we can have different songs. You will also find some examples of movement games that illustrate patterns. Perhaps you would like to teach one of them to the class as well.

Each kit will also have scraps of paper or cloth to make pattern art. Maybe your children would like to draw their own patterns. That would be great too. We will exhibit their work, along with their art creations from school, at the party.

Remember that everyday things that you do with your children build math concepts. Let them sort the laundry into like piles—all the shirts, socks, and so forth together. Help them to notice patterns indoors and outdoors and in clothing and wallpaper. When you go to the grocery store, point out that products are sorted and classified according to categories of food. They can help you unpack your groceries and sort them to put in cabinets.

Thank you for taking the time to help us with math concepts. We hope that they are fun for you as well. We would also welcome your ideas for projects. We will be in touch with you in the next few weeks about the party.

Sincerely,

Permission is granted by the publisher to reproduce this page.

Tear-Out Sheet 3

Math Party

Everyone Come—Art Exhibits, Games, and Songs

Baby-Sitting and Food

Date:

Dear Parents:

We are about to conclude our units on patterns and classifying and sorting. We hope you have enjoyed the activities that you have done at home with your child. We greatly appreciate your help. Children learn so much from doing things with their parents.

Now it is time to have a party to recognize all of the hard work that you and your children have done in the area of math. We have all learned through your efforts. Your whole family is invited, and transportation will be provided for anyone who needs it. Just drop us a note.

On _____ at _____ in the _____ at school, we will be having our math party. The event will include the beautiful artwork that you have done with your children. In addition, we will be singing the songs that we all learned and trying some movement activities. Thank you so much to those of you who volunteered to teach a song or a dance.

There will also be exhibits involving sorting and classifying, wonderful patterns made with blocks, and an exhibit of children's books, both fiction and nonfiction, that are about math concepts. The children will be cooking pasta in different shapes and making cookies in patterns. We will have plenty of food on hand for all of us to sample (and more prepared by our wonderful cook).

We thank you again for working with us and look forward to seeing you at the party. Please come and bring the whole family.

Sincerely,

Tear-Out Sheet 4

Group Observation—Mathematics Terms
Algebra

Date:

Center/Area:

Child's or Children's Names:

Math Terms Used (Record the terms taught to children on the left.)

	Accuracy		
	None at All	Some	Complete
1.	_____	_____	_____
2.	_____	_____	_____
3.	_____	_____	_____
4.	_____	_____	_____
5.	_____	_____	_____
6.	_____	_____	_____
7.	_____	_____	_____
8.	_____	_____	_____
9.	_____	_____	_____
10.	_____	_____	_____

Comments:

Permission is granted by the publisher to reproduce this page.

Tear-Out Sheet 5

Date: _____

Name: _____

Age of Child: _____

**Individual Evaluation: Assessing Children's Math Skills—
Basic Concepts of Algebra**

	Always	**Sometimes**	**Never**
Identifies patterns:			
In numbers	_____	_____	_____
In designs	_____	_____	_____
In music	_____	_____	_____
In movement	_____	_____	_____
Creates and explains patterns	_____	_____	_____
Repeats and extends patterns	_____	_____	_____
Describes quantitative changes in living things	_____	_____	_____
Describes qualitative changes in living things	_____	_____	_____
Sorts, classifies, and orders concrete objects by various attributes:			
Length	_____	_____	_____
Width	_____	_____	_____
Color	_____	_____	_____
Other	_____	_____	_____
Uses simple algebraic terminology	_____	_____	_____

Additional Comments:

Experience 3

Young Children Learn the Basic Concepts of Geometry

FOR THE TEACHER

◇ What You'll Need to Know

According to the National Council of Teachers of Mathematics (2000), preschool through second-grade geometry teaching begins with describing and naming shapes. Young students begin by using their own vocabulary to describe objects. Teachers must help students gradually to incorporate conventional terminology into their descriptions of two- and three-dimensional shapes. Yet, terminology should not be the focus of the program. Rather, mathematics learning builds on the curiosity and enthusiasm of children and grows naturally from their experiences. Adults can foster children's mathematical development by providing environments where thinking is encouraged, uniqueness is valued, and exploration is supported.

Children learn through exploring their world; thus, interests and everyday activities are natural vehicles for developing mathematical thinking. Shapes are all around us! Children learn early to be shape detectives at home, in the classroom, and on walking trips outside, where the teacher will most likely point out the octagonal stop sign and its importance.

Yet, quality learning results from both formal and informal experiences during the school year. Teachers will want to take advantage of incidental learnings, but they will also want to carefully plan explorations with problems, materials, and children's books that facilitate emergent concepts of geometry. The NCTM (2000) suggests that teachers challenge children to solve problems, support their efforts, and encourage their persistence.

◇ Key Concepts

- Geometric shapes are two- and three-dimensional.
- Two- and three-dimensional geometric shapes have multiple characteristics and properties to be analyzed.
- Investigations and predictions can be made about geometric shapes.
- Spatial reasoning and relationships are accomplished through geometry and other representational systems.
- Children's spatial sense is their awareness of themselves in relation to people and objects around them in space.
- Spatial visualization and reasoning can be used to solve problems.
- Geometry describes and classifies the physical world we live in.

◇ Goals and Objectives

Children will recognize, name, and compare two- and three-dimensional shapes.

Children will build with two- and three-dimensional shapes.

Children will compare and sort two- and three-dimensional shapes.

Children will draw two- and three-dimensional shapes and distinguish them from nonshapes.

Children will describe attributes and parts of two- and three-dimensional shapes.

Children will describe and name relative positions in space.

Children will describe and name direction and distance in space.

Experience 3 ◆ Young Children Learn the Basic Concepts of Geometry

Children will find and name locations with simple language such as "beside," "above," and "below."

Children will recognize geometric shapes and structures in the environment and specify their location.

◇ What You'll Need

There are few appropriate geometry books for teachers of young children who want to refresh their memories about this topic, and then apply it to a classroom for young children. The National Council of Teachers of Mathematics Standards contains many excellent ideas for supporting the teaching of geometry, but most of them are for the early elementary grades. One book that you might find helpful is *Navigating through Geometry in Prekindergarten–Grade 2* (with CD-Rom), (2001), by C. R. Findell, M. Small, M. Cavanagh, L. Dacey, C. E. Greenes, and L. J. Shellfield. Like its companion book in algebra, it demonstrates how some basic ideas of geometry can be introduced, developed, and extended. It deals with two- and three-dimensional shapes, and introduces methods to describe location and position.

Other books that may be helpful are

Read any good math lately? By D. J. Whitin and S. Wilde. (1992). Heinemann. This resource helps teachers find and use children's books in the classroom for mathematical learning.

The multicultural game book. By L. Orlando. (1993). Scholastic Professional Books. This book includes ideas for shapes that children can make and geometric principles they can learn from games.

Geometry from Africa: Mathematical and educational explorations. By P. Gerdes. (1999). Mathematical Association of America. The author shows how geometrical ideas are manifested in the work of African artisans. The large number of beautiful illustrations may inspire young artists to link their art with emergent concepts of geometry.

Preschoolers are learning to make mental images or pictures they can carry in their minds to refer to in learning concepts. Slightly older children are learning to form dynamic images that they can move or change. Yet children often have limiting ideas about shapes because of their inability to think abstractly. For example, a child may tell you that a square is not a square because it is too big. The teacher must challenge the child's thinking by pointing out a variety of examples—triangles that are long, skinny, and fat. The more young children work with geometric concepts, the more they can learn to explore spatial relations and experience mathematics. They are also ready to make and use simple maps and to describe their location in space and the location of other people and things that are important to them.

Children's Books

Burns, M. (1994). *The greedy triangle.* New York: Scholastic.

Carle, E. (1986). *The secret birthday message.* New York: Harper/Trophy.

Children's Television Workshop. (2000). *Cookie bakes up shapes.* New York Preschool Press. Time-Life Books.

Dodds, D. A. (1994). *The shape of things.* Cambridge, MA: Candlewick.

Grifalconi, V. (1986). *The village of round and square houses.* Boston: Little Brown.

Grover, M. (1996). *Circles and squares everywhere.* New York: Harcourt.

Hirst, R. & S. (1990). *My place in space.* London: The Watts Publishing Group.

Hoban, T. (1986). *Shapes, shapes, shapes.* New York: Greenwillow Books.

Hoban, T. (1996). *Circles, triangles, and squares.* New York: Greenwillow Books.

Santomero, A. C. (1998). *The shape detectives.* New York: Simon Spotlight, an Imprint of Simon and Schuster, Children's Publishing Division.

Serfozo, M. (1996). *There's a square: A book about shapes.* New York: Scholastic.

Seuss, Dr. (1988). *The shape of me and other stuff.* New York: Random House.

Silverstein, S. (1976). *The missing piece.* New York: Harper Collins Children's Books.

Other Things You'll Need

- Containers for sorting
- Large blocks in all shapes
- Plenty of room to build inside and outside
- Small blocks in various shapes for building, sorting, and manipulating
- Paper, drawing tools, collage materials, large butcher paper, and other art supplies
- Magazines and catalogs for collage
- Magazines and photographs featuring many shapes for examination
- Access to the outdoor environment to identify shapes in nature and in the neighborhood
- Straws and yarn
- Journals and clipboards for children to record observations
- Real and "play" maps for describing relative location and direction in space

Active experiences help children visualize their relative position in space.

- A geoboard with bands
- A set of tangrams for older children
- Large and small cartons for outside building and for examination. These may also be decorated by the children.
- A sand table or outdoor sandbox for building cities to assist with mapping and spatial skills

◇ **The Home-School Connection**

In their booklet on early mathematics for parents, *Early Childhood: Where Learning Begins—Mathematics,* the U.S. Department of Education suggests that parents ask children to think about and solve problems that arise in their everyday activities together. Through newsletters, bulletin boards, and special events at school, the teacher can convey more specific strategies for developing emergent geometry concepts and skills throughout the day. Things that parents can do to help their children learn geometry include the following:

1. Ask them to identify and describe different shapes, draw them in the air with their finger, or draw them on paper if available. Shapes are everywhere in the home and in the outside environment, so there are plenty of opportunities to discuss them and their attributes.

2. Allow children to have hands-on experiences with shapes. Blocks, boxes and containers, and puzzles provide opportunities for concrete exploration of shape concepts.

3. At lunchtime, or when preparing lunch for school, have children cut their sandwiches into different shapes and fit them together again.

4. Allow children to experience themselves in space. They can go around the house and begin to use words such as *under, over, through, into,* and *on top of* to describe their experience.

5. Outside, children can use large pieces of chalk or a rock to draw shapes on the sidewalk or in the dirt. This provides good practice in drawing and recognizing shapes.

Parents need not spend a great deal of extra time on these activities with children. As the day progresses, activities with shapes suggest themselves naturally.

◇ **Evaluating and Assessing Children's Learning**

Assessing children's emergent concepts of geometry and location in space will be a continuous activity done on an individual and group basis using

- observations of children's explorations and conversations
- small and large group discussions with students as they work individually and in groups

- structured interviews with students
- portfolios of children's work collected throughout the year
- children's self-evaluations, drawings, and dictated stories about geometry concepts
- children's math journals

The tear-out sheets on pages 97–98 at the end of this experience can be used at different intervals during the school year to chart growth in children's knowledge of emergent geometry concepts and to help you plan your curriculum on the basis of children's current understandings and your goals for the year.

FOR THE CHILDREN

In providing active experiences for children, we recognize that young children "do" geometry spontaneously in their lives and in their play. They make sense of the world around them by exploring shapes and patterns, drawing and creating geometric designs, and learning new vocabulary to name the things they see. Through the following active experiences, children can build on the strengths and interests that are already present.

According to the *Principles and Standards for School Mathematics* (NCTM, 2000), students should use their notions of geometric ideas to become more proficient in describing, representing, and navigating their environment. They should learn to represent two- and three-dimensional shapes through drawings, block constructions, dramatizations, and words. They should explore shapes by decomposing them and creating new ones. Their knowledge of direction and position should be refined through the use of spoken language to locate objects and by giving and following multistep directions (chapter 4, p. 43).

◇ Doing Geometry

◆ For younger children, pass around different shapes and have the children look at them and feel them with eyes open and closed. This will develop the idea that we can use our visual and tactile senses to identify shapes.

◆ Have children lie on the carpet and create the shapes they know with their bodies. Have two or three children create a shape using their bodies together.

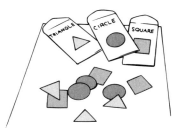

◆ Precut construction paper rectangles, squares, circles, trapezoids, and the like. Provide envelopes or containers with a representation of each form and the correct word for it. Have children sort the shapes into containers. Older children can cut their own shapes for various activities such as art, sorting games, and so on.

◆ To develop children's spatial sense, ask them to pretend they are flies on the ceiling. Have them create a map of the classroom using the precut construction paper forms. Have them add details to denote location. It is not expected that young children will reproduce perspective correctly, but this is a wonderful start in building mapping skills.

◆ Read *The Shape Detectives* by A. C. Santomero. Go on a shape walk. Have the children act as "shape detectives" and record the shapes they observe and where they

Experience 3 ◆ Young Children Learn the Basic Concepts of Geometry   91

were found. The teacher can assist as necessary by providing clues and helping children to record their findings. Be sure to take clipboards or journals along for children to draw or write their findings. Then graph or chart how many of each shape the children found. You may ask them to make predictions before the walk and compare them with the data.

◆ Using *The Shape Detectives,* ask the children to look around their houses and find lots of shapes. Ask parents to record how many and of what kind.

◆ Read *Cookie Bakes Up Shapes* from Sesame Street, Children's Television Worshop. Make dough with the children and have them make geometric shapes with cookie cutters. Also have them create free-form creative shapes with the dough. Bake the cookies and have the children try to identify the shapes before they eat them. Older children can participate in the baking process and watch the transformation of the dough. Younger children will enjoy seeing the shapes after baking. Parents may participate by sending in good, simple cookie recipes.

◆ Make or order round pizza. Let the children predict how many triangle pieces can be cut. Vary the size of the pieces. See how many triangles children can eat.

◆ Fold paper to make shapes. Fold a square to make a rectangle; fold a rectangle to make a triangle; fold a trapezoid to make a diamond.

◆ Have the children create shapes out of yarn and out of toothpicks. Compare them.

◆ Use catalogs or magazines to find examples of various shapes. First have children sort them. Then have a group of children put together a "How many shapes can you find?" collage.

◆ Read *Shapes, Shapes, Shapes* and *Circles, Triangles, and Squares* by T. Hoban. Have children identify the shapes on each page of the book. Chart their answers. They will probably have trouble discriminating among these complex patterns at first. Ask them to look closely for more shapes. Have children write a story about one of the books. Ask them to use "shape words" such as *circle, hexagon, oval, diamond, rectangle, square,* and *triangle.* There are some surprising shapes in the photographs. Ask them to use *heart, arc,* and *star* in the story.

◆ Create or add to a word wall using their new math vocabulary and the new shape and location words acquired in the study of geometry.

◆ Play a variation of "Simon Says" using position words (e.g., Simon says stand "between," go "under," climb "over"). Have children try out as many space words as they can. Examples are *near/far, inside/outside, in front of/behind, next to* or *beside, above/below.*

◆ Have a treasure hunt. Give children paper bags (one for each) and ask them to find things of a certain shape that you have put around the room or outside. They may also find shapes in nature to bring into the classroom and exhibit.

◆ Read *My Place in Space* by R. and S. Hirst. Ask children what they would include as their address on earth. What could they add besides the street, town, and country?

Have children create a complex address for the location of other things such as a tree, a building, or the school.

- Have students construct a triangle using cut straws and kite string. Then suggest they cut the straws to different lengths and string them. Sometimes they will not get a triangle. Students should try to predict whether a particular combination of lengths will form a triangle. Have children explore shapes that are geometric and those that are not. On a chart or diagram, illustrate geometric and nongeometric shapes.

- Have children create shape pictures using a specified number of circles, triangles, and rectangles. Encourage them to be creative.

- Read *The Shape of Me and Other Stuff* by Dr. Seuss. Have the children, using butcher paper and markers, make life-size copies of themselves with partners. Have them draw themselves twice and cut out the body images. When they have finished coloring in a face and adding clothes, have them each staple the two pieces together, leaving a small opening. Help them stuff their figures with newspapers and finish stapling. Display the three-dimensional figures around the room. Discuss with the class why people, animals, and objects have some of the shapes they do.

- Have children build simple maps with landscape toys such as schools, houses, cars, and trees. Have them examine their maps and ask them what they think the relative distance is between the various places.

- Have children find a hidden object by using a simple map of the classroom that you have created.

- Have a well-equipped block area with blocks of all kinds and shelves on which to sort them when play is over. Label the shelves to facilitate shape vocabulary. Give children plenty of time to create complex block play. (This will increase with age.) Add directional signs and books about construction to the area to inspire play. Ask and answer questions about how shapes work in the construction process.

- Try having the children dance shapes and patterns. Use the cassette or disc *Dancing Numerals* by Rosemary Hallum. Counting, geometric shapes, patterns, and simple addition and subtraction are included with the appropriate physical movements. Available from Educational Activities, Inc. (See resources list at the end of this book.)

◇ **Reflecting**

Children can organize their experiences by using a large area of the classroom to display their journals, charts, artwork, and stories. Large structures can be left up for a period of days for other children to examine. The children might invite other members of the school community to admire their building with shapes. Word walls should remain to remind children to use their new vocabulary to label their work and in conversation about emergent concepts of geometry. Display their three-dimensional figures and shape pictures.

Have a party for family members to view and experiment with active math experiences involving two- and three-dimensional shapes. Serve sandwiches and cookies made in shapes. Create simple sorting games for younger siblings. Be sure to have your read-

Experience 3 ◆ Young Children Learn the Basic Concepts of Geometry

ing center well stocked with children's books relating to mathematics for parents to examine and read.

◇ Extending and Expanding to the Primary Grades

Children in the early primary grades can do the following:

- Use interactive computer programs for activities in which students put together or take apart shapes. The National Council of Teachers of Mathematics has electronic examples that can be used for different age groups (see resources list at the end of this book). One interactive sequence is called "Investigating the Concept of Triangle and Properties of Polygons." It uses interactive geoboards to help students identify shapes, describe their properties, and develop spatial sense. In the second part, students make and compare various polygons, describing the properties of the shapes they create.

- Apply transformations and use symmetry to analyze mathematical situations. Students can recognize and create shapes that have symmetry and recognize and apply slides, flips, and turns in shapes. They can use pattern blocks to create designs with line and rotational symmetry, or paper cutouts, paper folding, and mirrors to investigate symmetry.

- Learn about geometric properties by combining or cutting apart shapes to form new shapes.

- Refine and extend concepts of position in space by developing map skills that include making route maps and using simple coordinates to locate the school on a city map. Some computer programs allow students to navigate through mazes or maps.

- Apply strategies in problem solving such as predicting the results of changing a shape's position but not its size or shape.

- Think more abstractly about shape concepts. For example, children can read *The Greedy Triangle* by M. Burns. In this story about a triangle that is unhappy with its shape and keeps asking the local Shapeshifter to give it more sides and angles, there are many important jobs for triangles, quadrilaterals, pentagons, and hexagons. Let students choose which of the four they would like to be and explain orally and in writing the reasons for their choice.

- Understand that shapes have their background in historical tradition, folktales, and ancient cultures. For example, tangrams are ancient Chinese puzzle pieces of geometric shapes still used today by adults and children to design beautiful and unique pictures. A good book to accompany an experience with tangrams is *Grandfather Tang's Story* by A. Tompert.

- Appreciate the beauty of a poem about shapes. Read *The Missing Piece* by Shel Silverstein to young elementary school students. Discuss the possibility that everyone needs something to make them whole (a better person, a smarter person, and so on). Have children discuss what they might be missing and what they could do to find their missing piece.

- Build a larger and more complex vocabulary pertaining to geometric and spatial concepts.

- Learn more complex classification systems for two- and three-dimensional shapes.

◇ Documenting Children's Learning

A web can document the concepts, learnings, skills, and attitudes that children have developed through their active experiences with geometry. Teachers will want the children to take part in generating various sections of the web. This will assist with reflection and recall. Parents might wish to add to a general web or create their own webs based on the things they have learned about geometry with their children. An activity for the party might be the creation of several webs to hang in the classroom as a reminder of the integrated learning that took place.

Child-made bulletin boards, minimuseums, word walls, Venn diagrams, and labeled displays all document children's new concepts of geometry.

Tear-Out Sheet 1

Date:

Dear Parents:

Shapes (geometric and nongeometric) are everywhere. As part of our continuing math curriculum, we are working on basic concepts in geometry. Simply, we will be doing almost anything possible with shapes from identifying them in the classroom and outside, to making them with our bodies, to baking cookies with various geometric shapes. We will undertake a lot of art activities using shapes. We are also working on basic concepts of space that the children will translate later into map skills. At this point they will attempt to create simple maps in the sand, with blocks, and on paper.

There are many things that you can do to help us at school and at home. We would love to have you come in and volunteer in the classroom whenever you can. Please let us know a bit ahead so we will be prepared for your visit. But if you can't fit a visit into school hours, please help us reinforce your children's beginning concepts of geometry.

At home, you can point out shapes to your children, and encourage them to point them out to you. When you go on a walk, encourage them to look for shapes on buildings or in the park.

To help with space skills, try to emphasize "location words" such as "beside," "above," "under," and "over." Help your children to locate themselves in space with such observations as, "Look. You are standing between Daddy and Grandma."

Thank you for taking the time to help us with math concepts. We hope that they are fun for you as well. We will be in touch with you in the next few weeks about a shapes and space party for all of our children and their families.

Sincerely,

Geometry Party (Shapes and Space)

Everyone Come

Games, Treasure Hunts, Music, and Food

Baby-Sitting Provided

Date:

Dear Parents:

We are about to conclude our unit on beginning concepts in geometry. We hope you have enjoyed the activities that you have done at home with your child. We greatly appreciate your help. Children learn so much from doing things with their parents.

Now it is time to have a party to recognize all of the hard work that you and your children have done in the area of math. We have all learned through your efforts. Your whole family is invited, and transportation will be provided for anyone who needs it. Just drop us a note.

On _____ at _____ in the _____ at school, we will be having a geometry party. Shapes and maps will be everywhere. Children's artwork using shapes will be displayed, as well as posters listing the math words that we have learned. There will be music and movement activities using shapes and a treasure hunt for younger children with prizes for all.

The children will be cutting out sandwiches using geometric shapes and baking cookies as well. We will have plenty of food on hand for all of us to sample (and pizza prepared by our wonderful cook).

We thank you again for working with us and look forward to seeing you at the party. Please come and bring the whole family.

Sincerely,

Tear-Out Sheet 3

Group Observation—Beginning Geometry Terms

Date:

Center/Area:

Child's or Children's Names:

Math Terms Used (Record terms taught to children on the left.)

	Accuracy		
	None at All	**Some**	**Complete**
1.	_____	_____	_____
2.	_____	_____	_____
3.	_____	_____	_____
4.	_____	_____	_____
5.	_____	_____	_____
6.	_____	_____	_____
7.	_____	_____	_____
8.	_____	_____	_____
9.	_____	_____	_____
10.	_____	_____	_____

Comments:

Permission is granted by the publisher to reproduce this page.

Tear-Out Sheet 4

Date: _____
Name: _____
Age of Child: _____

**Individual Evaluation: Assessing Children's Math Skills—
Basic Concepts of Geometry**

	Always	Sometimes	Never
Recognizes shapes	_____	_____	_____
Names shapes	_____	_____	_____
Compares two- and three-dimensional shapes	_____	_____	_____
Builds with two- and three-dimensional shapes	_____	_____	_____
Draws two- and three-dimensional shapes	_____	_____	_____
Distinguishes shapes from nonshapes	_____	_____	_____
Describes attributes of two- and three-dimensional shapes	_____	_____	_____
Describes parts of two- and three-dimensional shapes	_____	_____	_____
Describes relative positions in space	_____	_____	_____
Names relative positions in space	_____	_____	_____
Describes direction in space	_____	_____	_____
Names direction in space	_____	_____	_____
Describes distance in space	_____	_____	_____
Finds and names locations in space with simple language such as "beside"	_____	_____	_____
Recognizes geometric shapes and structures in the environment and specifies their location	_____	_____	_____

Additional Comments:

Permission is granted by the publisher to reproduce this page.

EXPERIENCE 4

Young Children Learn the Basic Concepts of Measurement

FOR THE TEACHER

◇ What You'll Need to Know

Things to measure are everywhere: How tall is that block tower? How far is it to the end of the classroom? How big is Billy? Is Juan bigger? How do we know? How heavy is the water in that container? The sand in that cup? How many small cups will it take to fill the large cup? How much time will it take to go on our walk? How much time before snack, before the parents come to get their children? How old is Grandpa? Young children are infinitely interested in finding the answers to the many questions they have about things that can be measured, such as their own height and weight.

In the early childhood years, they should (1) begin to understand the measurable attributes of objects and (2) be able to choose and apply techniques and tools to find out the answers to questions of measurement. They begin by looking at, touching, or directly comparing objects. Teachers will want to guide students by making the resources for measuring available, planning formal and informal opportunities to measure, encouraging students to explain and discuss their findings, and asking important questions to facilitate their thinking and concept development.

The National Council of Teachers of Mathematics (2000) suggests, in the measurement standard for grades Pre-K–2, that measurement is one of the most widely used applications of mathematics. For young children, informal measurement experiences both teach important everyday skills and develop measurement concepts and processes that will be formalized and expanded in later years. A foundation in measurement concepts involves direct hands-on experiences with comparing objects, counting units of measurement (both formal and informal), and using a variety of tools. Teachers may first want to assist children in measuring the length of an object with string or rods. Later they can introduce standard measurement tools such as rulers and scales.

Young children have difficulty with concepts of time. Conventional clocks pose many obstacles. Although some young children will learn to use them to tell time, they have egocentric beliefs about time that hinder the development of basic concepts, such as the notion that time intervals are not constant—that they can catch up with their brother in age—or that someone is older because they are taller. The important thing for the teacher to emphasize is patterns in time, such as the progression through minutes, hours, days, weeks, and months. A classroom calendar may help children to see time concepts more concretely, especially if each day is blocked in with a concrete activity or activities that children can remember. When basic concepts of time are tied to concrete things or experiences, children begin to understand them: "We will have snack after we clean up the art center."

So while measurement concepts are in some ways easy to teach, they pose a challenge for young children. They have particular difficulty in making the transition from informal to more formal understandings. Teachers may want to make conversational assessments with individual or groups of children to see how well they are internalizing concepts.

◇ Key Concepts

- Things may be compared with respect to length, area, capacity, weight, and time.
- Objects may be ordered according to these attributes.
- Length concepts involve how long, how high, how far, and how wide.
- Area concepts require that children look at more than one measurable dimension.

Experience 4 ♦ Young Children Learn the Basic Concepts of Measurement

- Capacity and volume have many everyday applications, as with sand and water.
- Weight can be compared using balance scales or regular scales.
- Time is relative for young children and is best taught through everyday routines and conversations.
- Measurement varies with the size of the unit used to make the measurement.
- Accurate measurement depends on proper use of an appropriate tool.
- Estimation is useful in building basic concepts when things such as a million cannot be measured.

◇ Goals and Objectives

Goals and objectives for young children in the area of measurement involve both understandings and applications. According to NCTM (2002), depending on the age of the child, instructional programs for young children in grades Pre-K–2 should enable all students to

- *understand* measurable attributes of objects and the units, systems, and processes of measurement.
- *apply* appropriate techniques, tools, and formulas to determine measurements. While adults know instinctively that they will need a scale to measure weight or a clock to measure time, young children have not had sufficient experiences with the tools of measurement to make correct choices.

Thus, in the math program for young children, activities will be formulated to help children to begin to do the following:

Children will recognize the attributes of length, volume, weight, area, and time.

Children will compare and order objects according to these attributes.

Children will understand how to measure things using both standard and nonstandard units.

Children will be able to select the appropriate unit and tool for the attribute being measured.

Children will measure with multiple copies of units of the same size such as long unit blocks.

Children will use repetition of a single unit to measure something larger than the unit.

Children will use standard tools such as rulers and scales to measure.

Children will make comparisons and estimates.

Children will learn a beginning measurement vocabulary.

Children will use measurement to solve everyday school and home problems.

Linear measurement receives the most emphasis in the early childhood classroom. Length concepts involve how long, how high, how far, how wide, and how far around something is, but young children need to be introduced to the other measurable attributes of objects to begin to form basic concepts of measurement.

◇ **What You'll Need**

There are some activity books that contain measurement experiences, but again it is difficult to find good books for teachers to cement their concepts of measurement and help with in-depth, concept-building experiences for children. The following may be helpful, and activities for kindergartners may be adapted for younger preschool children:

Little kids, powerful problem solvers: Math stories from a kindergarten classroom. By A. G. Andrews and P. R. Trafton. (2002). Heinemann. One story describes the first lesson in a yearlong focus on measurement as a theme. The goal is for children to make sense of mathematics by rooting it in concrete experiences, using rice and water to investigate capacity and examine the behavior of liquids and solids.

Experiences in math for young children. By R. Charlesworth. (2000). Delmar (a division of Thomson Learning.) The author covers fundamental concepts and skills for prekindergarten through third grade. There is a section on measurement that is tied to the NCTM standards.

Mathematics for the young child. Edited by J. Payne. (1990). National Council of Teachers of Mathematics. Activities and suggestions are presented for teacher educators and teachers in preschool through grade 4.

Math and literature (k–3). M. Burns, (1993). Marilyn Burns Education Associates. This book has a very good lesson on measurement using *How Big Is a Foot?* by R. Myller. (See children's books list.)

Math links series: Measuring. By P. Patilla. (1999). Heinemann First Library Series. This books links measurement with everyday occurrences. The left-hand page introduces the concept, and the right-hand page shows the concept at work in the real world. The teacher will appreciate the glossary and reference list for further reading.

Children's Books

Adler, D. A. (1999). *How tall, how short, how far away.* New York: Holiday House.

Anno, M. (translation and special contents of this book copyrighted in 1987 by Philomel Books, a division of Putnam & Grosset Group). *Anno's math games.*

Carle, E. (1969). *The very hungry caterpillar.* London: Hamish Hamilton.

Carle, E. (1996). *The grouchy ladybug.* Old Tappan, NJ: Scott Foresman (Pearson K–12).

Fowler, R. (1993). *Ladybug on the move.* New York: Harcourt.

Hoban, T. (1985). *Is it larger? Is it smaller?* New York: Greenwillow.

Hutchins, P. (1970). *Clocks and more clocks.* New York: Macmillan.

Marvelous math: A book of poems. (1997). Selected by L. B. Hopkins. New York: Simon & Schuster Books for Young Readers.

Meeks, S. (2002). *Drip drop.* New York: HarperTrophy.

Murphy, S. (1997). *Betcha!* New York: HarperCollins.

Myller, R. (1991). *How big is a foot?* Old Tappan, NJ: Scott Foresman (Pearson K–12).

Schwartz, D. A. (1985). *How much is a million?* New York: Mulberry Books (an imprint of William Morrow & Co.)

Shaw, C. G. (1988). *It looked like spilt milk.* New York: HarperTrophy.

Wing, R. W. (1963). *What is big?* New York: Holt, Rinehart and Winston.

Other Things You'll Need

- Nonstandard units of measurement such as lengths of string, blocks, and paper clips
- Standard units of measurement such as rulers, tablespoons, various sizes of containers (quart and so on), cups of various sizes, different types of scales (bathroom, balance—a two-sided scale that has containers on either side—kitchen, and produce—the kind that hangs)
- Water and sand tables
- Water, sand, rice, and other materials to work with volume
- Different types of clocks such as digital, conventional, watches
- An hourglass
- Math journals
- Construction paper, chart paper, markers, paper plates, fasteners, and other art materials
- Objects for weighing. You might want to include a wide variety of objects that vary not only in weight but size as well. It is also good to have smaller objects that are heavy and larger objects that are light so that children can determine the weight by measuring, not by the size of the object. Objects to weigh may come from indoors or out-of-doors.
- Ingredients for cooking
- Clear containers full of things such as marbles or pennies for children to estimate amount
- A large classroom calendar and various stickers and art materials to mark the sequence of time

◇ **The Home-School Connection**

In its booklet on early mathematics, the U.S. Department of Education has many suggestions for practicing measurement with children. Teachers can convey these ideas and others to parents through newsletters, bulletin boards, meetings, and special school activities. Another excellent source of activities is the Family Math Program at the Lawrence Hall of Science, University of California, Berkeley. Their new book, *Spark Your Child's Success in Math and Science: Practical Advice for Parents* by J. Barber, N. Parizeau, and L. Bergman, comes with a companion Web site. The following are some ideas for parents:

1. Keep a record of your children's height by marking the wall lightly with erasable pencil and measuring height every month. Young children love seeing how big they are getting and predicting how big they will be in several months.

2. Let children use informal units of measure like footsteps or blocks. Let them pick from an array of possible measurement units. Discuss "how many."

3. Many daily activities involve measurement: cooking, gardening, grocery shopping, and repairing things around the house. Talk to your children about what you are doing and what tools you are using to accomplish the task. For example, the cake needs "three teaspoons of vanilla." "How many cups of sugar do you think we will need?"

4. If possible, have children help you with measurement chores by holding the ruler or filling the cup.

5. Although parents should understand that they should not attempt to teach young children conventional concepts of time, there are some activities they can do to build the foundation for later concept development:

   - Help children to learn that some activities take longer than others: "Does it take longer to drive to school or to the grocery store? What do you think?"

   - Relate units of time to counting by using a watch to time events and counting the ticks of the second hand.

   - Have lots of discussion about time using relational terms such as "before bed" or "after dinner."

   - Have children estimate how many candies are in a jar or how many minutes it will take to walk to the park. Sometimes the estimates can be tested against the actual number and other times the number will be too large, but children will learn to make an educated guess.

   - Use math vocabulary such as "about the same," "near," "approximately," "more than," and "fewer than."

Teachers will want to make it clear to parents that they need not create "homework" about measurement for their children. In the course of a day, many activities will suggest themselves, and children will obtain practice with measurement concepts. Have a party for your students and their family members using measurement as the theme. Decorate the classroom with children's displays, journals, a large calendar, and a word wall. Use *Anno's Math Games* by Mitsumasa Anno to challenge parents, grandparents, and older siblings to practice their math or learn different concepts.(See the tear-out sheet on p. 111.)

◇ Evaluating and Assessing Children's Learning

Assessing emergent concepts of measurement will be a continuous activity done on an individual and group basis using

- observations of children's problem solving and conversations
- small and large group discussions with students as they work individually and in groups
- structured interviews with students
- portfolios of children's work collected throughout the year
- children's self-evaluations, drawings, and dictated stories about measurement concepts
- children's math journals

The tear-out sheets on pages 112–113 at the end of this experience can be used at different intervals during the school year to chart growth in children's knowledge of

Experience 4 ◆ Young Children Learn the Basic Concepts of Measurement

emergent measurement concepts, and to help you plan your curriculum on the basis of children's current understandings and your goals for the year.

FOR THE CHILDREN

According to the *Principles and Standards for School Mathematics* (NCTM, 2000), children should begin to develop an understanding of attributes by looking at, touching, or directly comparing objects. They can identify which of two objects is heavier by lifting them or compare their shoe sizes by putting them side by side. These emergent experiences with measurement build to more formal concepts of measurement in the early elementary school years.

◇ Measuring

- Discuss how to measure the length of the classroom walls, tables, and desks, or how to measure the distance from the door to the closet by using students' own two feet and counting the number of steps. Have students perform several measurements. Make a measurement chart or have students record measurements in their math journals (with your help). You may want to post the results on a bulletin board or hang them from hangers near the objects measured. Note and explain that the measurements will be relative depending on the size of the child and his or her feet.

- Following from the previous activity, ask the children to identify some other materials or objects that could be used to measure length. They may come up with blocks, cubes, yarn, paper clips, and so forth. You may want to make a word wall of nonstandard units that can be used for measuring.

- Provide children with a variety of nonstandard units of measurement. Make a list of possible things to measure, and allow students to formulate their own questions such as "Which is longer, the desk or the table?" Students may measure using one nonstandard unit or several. Have them make comparisons. For example, "How many pieces of yarn did it take to measure the table? How many blocks?"

- Provide standard units for measuring length, such as rulers and tape measures. Have the students try them on various objects as they wish. Younger children may not always use standard units correctly, such as leaving spaces between ruler measurements. The teacher can help, but facility with standard units will come with time.

- Make a chart of "guiding questions" (*illuminations.nctm.org/lessonplans/prek-2/measurement/index.html*). They would include

    Which object was the longest?

    Which object was the shortest?

    Which object was the tallest?

    Which object was the widest?

    Which object was the most narrow?

    Ask children for other questions. Hang them in the classroom as a reminder of which attributes children may want to investigate.

◆ Make a card with a matching picture for each of the following relational words:

Large	Small
Long	Short
Tall	Short
Wide	Narrow
Fat	Thin
Heavy	Light
Old	New
High	Low

Gather a small group of children. Have children pick a card and name something that fits the card. To ensure that children have the right idea, restrict the items named to objects or people in the room. Older children can play this game without assistance from the teacher and extend their answers to objects in their homes or to family members.

◆ Create an area on the hardtop in the play yard. Ask the children to put all of the wheeled vehicles in the area. How many vehicles does it take to fill the area? You may use any other large objects, such as cartons and other outdoor play equipment. Record the answers. Rope off an area on the carpet in the classroom. Find out how many children it takes to fill the area. Chart the answer. Change the size of the areas from time to time.

◆ Plan a cooking project with the children based upon their interests. Make a chart with the number of standard units of each ingredient that will be needed. Use pictorial representations as well. Assemble the standard units and have the children assist you in combining the ingredients. Talk about the process as you work. If you make something such as fruit salad, each child may assemble his or her own portion using spoons of various sizes. Note: Cooking may give you the opportunity to discuss the continuum of hot–cold, which is also measurable with young children, but safety must be strongly considered.

Parents can assist children with measurement concepts by including them in daily cooking activities.

- Read *The Grouchy Ladybug* by Eric Carle. Ask the children what the ladybug was doing each hour of the day. The book contains a ladybug clock, which each child can reproduce with paper plates and fasteners for the hands. Telling time with clocks is hard for young children, but they may want to discuss what the ladybug did in the morning and at night. Have a variety of clocks around the classroom for children to examine.

- Read *The Very Hungry Caterpillar* by Eric Carle. The "tiny and very hungry caterpillar" eats his way through the days in the process of becoming a "beautiful butterfly." Children may slowly get the names of the days of the week in order, but more importantly they will see the progression through time in this event. Encourage the children to use measurement vocabulary as you discuss the book.

- Place containers of various sizes in the water table. Let children experiment freely with filling containers. Then pose some questions such as "How many small containers will it take to fill this large one?" "How heavy will the large one be when we fill it?" Record the answers on chart paper or in math journals. In the summer, it is easy and fun to have children experiment with water volume using a small wading pool. Be sure to observe safety rules.

- Place containers of various sizes at the sand table or use large containers filled with rice. Allow children to experiment freely with filling and refilling containers. Then pose questions for them to answer as previously suggested. Record answers on chart paper or in math journals.

- Create a corner of the classroom for weighing objects of all kinds. For example, children may take a walk and collect rocks of various sizes. They will want to see how much they weigh and compare the weights of various rocks. Children may decide what things in the room they would like to weigh and compare. Include a variety of scales. Children may want to weigh themselves or each other on a bathroom scale or ingredients for a cooking project on a kitchen scale. You may want to use a KWL chart to find out what students want to know about weight and what they learned through their measurement activities. Also use vocabulary such as "heavier" and "lighter."

- Create a large classroom calendar. Make sure students observe the progression through the day and week by recording what happened at different times. Have students participate by adding their own drawings or stories to explain what they did on different days. Again, children may not get the sequence of the days of the week, but they should feel their progression through time as the weeks and months go by.

- Read *How Much Is a Million?* by David M. Schwartz. This book, with its charming illustrations, allows children to see the vastness of numbers like a million or a billion. Of course, they will never be able to count that high, but the book provides some concrete examples such as "If a goldfish bowl were big enough for a million goldfish . . . it would be large enough to hold a whale." The many, many little stars give young children an opportunity to see just "how many" objects can be. Older children can certainly profit more directly from this book. The author provides his notes at the end.

- If you decide to house animals in the classroom, there are many measurement activities associated with their care and feeding. First, children will need to measure

in cups the required amount of food for each animal each day. Next, children will want to chart the growth of classroom animals, particularly if they reproduce. Both standard and nonstandard measuring tools can be used to measure the babies. Then the results may be recorded on chart paper. Teachers may suggest that children compare the growth of different animals or watch how fast and how big they grow. Older children can use simple graphs to represent the animals' progress.

- Plant seeds as a small group or large group project with many choices for how children will undertake their own experiment. The teacher may want to have a discussion with the children first and chart the types of seeds that will be needed, how many, the type of soil, and the type of containers. Sun and water must be considered. Measure and chart changes in the plants as they grow. Children may use measuring implements to see how tall their plants are growing. The several types of plants may be compared. Younger children may draw pictures to indicate the changes; older children will want to keep a record of the plants' growth over time in their math journals.

◇ Extending and Expanding to the Primary Grades

Children in the early primary grades can do the following:

- Use their new vocabulary and knowledge of standard measures to understand the world. Introduce a unit on measurement by reading the poem "Take a Number" by Mary O' Neill in *Marvelous Math: A Book of Poems*. This poem asks children to visualize a world without mathematics: no rulers or scales, inches or feet, prices or weights, days or nights—"Wouldn't it be awful to live like that?" Ask children to write a story about a world without math. Or make a chart of all the things in the world that are related to math. The chart may be done over time with one or two words added each day.

- Build a larger and more complex vocabulary pertaining to measurement concepts. Make a word wall of all the things in the world that are related to math. You might want to list words under the headings of length, volume, weight, area, and time. And another wall can list tools of measurement such as rulers, scales of various types, yardsticks, measuring cups, and the like.

- Understand units of measurement that are different from our own. Read *How Tall, How Short* by David A. Adler. Using that book as a basis, you can

  help children to figure out their height using the units of measure of ancient Egypt—digits, palms, spans, and cubits. The book illustrates each unit. Compare children's heights.

  have children measure the length of the hall or the classroom using paces (measures used in ancient Rome). Compare answers. Then try another unit of measurement.

  measure things around the classroom using the customary system (based on Roman measures) and the metric system. Have children try this out as a home activity and bring in their findings. Chart the various measurements. Analyze the data and create a display.

- Understand that math problems can be difficult, but enjoy the challenge of solving math problems. Read *Math Curse* by Jon Scieszka and Lane Smith, and let older children find out just how many math problems they can have if they "think of almost everything as a math problem."

- Use *Anno's Math Games* by Mitsumasa Anno to find the answers to a multitude of math problems through a game format. Parents will also enjoy working with their children using this book or trying it for themselves.

◇ Documenting Children's Learning

A Web can document the concepts, learnings, skills, and attitudes that children have developed through their active experiences with measurement. Teachers will want the children to take part in generating various sections of the web. This will assist with reflection and recall. Parents might wish to add to a general web or create their own webs based on the measurement activities they have undertaken with their children. An activity for the party might be the creation of several webs to hang in the classroom as a reminder of the integrated learning that took place.

Child-made bulletin boards, labeled displays, word walls, Venn diagrams, and math journals all document children's new concepts of measurement.

Date:

Dear Parents:

We are ready for another math unit. We will be working on basic measurement concepts. Although we always read and talk about measurement, we will be concentrating our efforts on children's understanding of the attributes of length, volume, weight, area, and time. There are many things that you can do to help us at school and at home. We would love to have you come and volunteer in the classroom whenever you can. Please let us know a bit ahead so we will be prepared for your visit. But if you can't fit a visit into school hours, please help us reinforce your child's emerging concepts of measurement.

We know that your children would love to be measured and weighed if you haven't already done that. You can chart their growth. How excited they'll be to see that they've grown an inch!

Suggest that your children measure things around your home. You don't need a ruler or tape measure. Try pieces of string or yarn or long blocks. Later you can provide "real" measurement tools. You can also talk to them about how long it takes to do some chores or to drive to the doctor's office. You can ask them to estimate which things take longer than others. They will probably have trouble reading the clock now, but they can understand what comes "before" and "after."

When you are cooking, allow your children to measure the ingredients using whatever measurement units the recipe calls for. Ask them to compare "how much salt" with "how much flour."

Encourage your children to illustrate their observations in their math journals. Perhaps they can dictate sentences to you about their measurement activities.

Thank you.

Sincerely,

Measurement Party

Games, Exhibits, and Prizes for Everyone

Everyone Come

Baby-Sitting and Food Provided

Date:

Dear Parents:

We are about to conclude our unit on measurement. We hope you have enjoyed the activities that you have done at home with your child. We greatly appreciate your help. Children learn so much from doing things with their parents.

Now it is time to have a party to recognize all of the hard work that you and your children have done in the area of math. We have all learned through your efforts. Your whole family is invited, and transportation will be provided for anyone who needs it. Just drop us a note.

On _____ at _____ in the _____ at school, we will be having a party based on the theme of measurement. Come see how our seeds have grown and try our measurement center with all kinds of scales and objects to weigh. See if you can guess which things are heavier or lighter. Try measuring the length of the classroom by using your feet to walk it. Try some of the games in the book *Anno's Math Games*. Let's see if you can spot the answers. Posters listing the measurement words that we have learned will be on exhibit.

The children will be measuring and cooking, so we will have plenty of food on hand for all of us to sample (and more prepared by our wonderful cook).

We thank you again for working with us and look forward to seeing you at the party. Please come and bring the whole family.

Sincerely,

Tear-Out Sheet 3

Group Observation—Mathematics Terms

Date:

Center/Area of the Room:

Child's or Children's Names:

Math Terms Used (Record the terms taught to children on the left.)

	Accuracy		
	Not at All	**Some**	**Complete**
1.	_____	_____	_____
2.	_____	_____	_____
3.	_____	_____	_____
4.	_____	_____	_____
5.	_____	_____	_____
6.	_____	_____	_____
7.	_____	_____	_____
8.	_____	_____	_____
9.	_____	_____	_____
10.	_____	_____	_____

Comments:

Tear-Out Sheet 4

Date: _____

Name: _____

Age of Child: _____

Individual Evaluation: Assessing Children's Math Skills—Measurement

	Always	Sometimes	Never
Recognizes the attribute of length	_____	_____	_____
Recognizes the attribute of volume	_____	_____	_____
Recognizes the attribute of weight	_____	_____	_____
Recognizes the attribute of area	_____	_____	_____
Recognizes the attribute of time	_____	_____	_____
Compares and orders objects according to			
Length	_____	_____	_____
Volume	_____	_____	_____
Weight	_____	_____	_____
Area	_____	_____	_____
Has emergent concepts of time—what comes "before," "after"	_____	_____	_____
Understands how to measure things using nonstandard units	_____	_____	_____
Understands how to measure things using standard units	_____	_____	_____
Is able to select the appropriate tool for the attribute being measured	_____	_____	_____
Makes comparisons and estimates	_____	_____	_____
Has a beginning measurement vocabulary	_____	_____	_____
Uses measurement to solve everyday home and school problems	_____	_____	_____

Additional Comments:

Permission is granted by the publisher to reproduce this page.

Checklist for Choosing Math Books for Young Children

- Is it a good book? Would I read this book to the children even if I weren't choosing it for a math lesson?
- Does the book stimulate curiosity? Will the children be inspired to do their own authentic investigations as a result of reading this book?
- Can the children make connections with the book? Are they familiar with some concepts so they can "launch" from there?
- Is the book contrived or are the math connections a natural part of the story or nonfictional presentation?
- Is the information accurate?
- Does the author use interesting details?
- Does the author acknowledge expert advisors?
- Is the book well organized with a clear structure?
- Is it easy to find information?
- Are there useful features such as an index, a table of contents, a glossary, and suggestions for other books and resources on the topic?
- Does the book have an appealing layout and design?
- Do photographs, diagrams, graphics, and other illustrations add to, explain, and extend information?
- Can the content and the language be understood by the intended audience?

Experience 5

Data Description, Organization, Representation, and Analysis

FOR THE TEACHER

◇ What You'll Need to Know

"Data analysis in the early childhood curriculum? Are you sure? I took statistics in college, but I'm not teaching it to young children," one teacher said. Of course young children have no need to understand statistics. Further, researchers claim that the "question of when and how many of the central conceptual structures of probability and statistics should be introduced in the elementary and middle grades" (NRC, 2001, p. 294) remains unanswered.

Regardless, if young children are actively involved in the study of their world, they will need to know how to collect, describe, organize, represent, and analyze their findings. In the process of doing so, they are becoming familiar with the ideas of statistics and probability. Further, Clements (1999) describes how very young children like working with substantial mathematics ideas. These inner-city minority children were self-motivated to investigate what numbers mean and how they work, leading Clements to conclude that there may be no better time to introduce substantial mathematical concepts such as data description, organization, representation, and analysis.

For example, a group of 3- and 4-year-olds studied their play yard. They were observed describing the play equipment in the yard. "The slide is the biggest," said one child. "It is not," said another. "It's tallest; the boat is the biggest." Each child was given a toss-away camera to take pictures of the play yard. After the photos were developed, the children organized them into different groups and, with the teacher, created a mural of "Our Play Yard." The children then took a survey to find out which piece of equipment was the most popular, and the teacher graphed their findings. Talking about their findings, the children concluded that the boat was very popular, followed by the fort/slide/swing center, and then the sand and water areas. The point is that young children's firsthand experiences with their here-and-now world naturally lead to using ideas of data description, organization, representation, and analysis.

Children do not automatically come to the preschool with the ability to argue over what is largest or tallest, to talk about their findings, or to graph them. The group of children studying their play yard had been exposed to making collections, counting them, and comparing them. The vocabulary of mathematics—tallest, shortest, and so on—had been introduced and reinforced daily. Further, these children were used to describing their world in pictorial or other representational forms.

◇ Key Concepts

- The study of statistics involves collecting, organizing, and sorting data.
- Concepts of labeling and scaling are crucial to data representation.
- Data can be described through graphs, tables, and lists.
- The process of analyzing and interpreting data involves recognition of patterns or trends, and gaining information from graphs.
- In the process of organizing data, children make inferences or predictions, and have initial experiences with probability.

◇ Goals and Objectives

Children will collect, organize, and sort data.

Children will begin to label information collected and develop an understanding of scale.

Children will organize data through pictures, graphs, tables, lists, and so on.

Children will gain meaning from graphs, tables, and lists by being able to find more/less; most/least; tallest/lowest; none, same, all; longest/shortest; fewer, least, all; higher/taller.

◇ What You'll Need

Great graphing. By L. Martin and M. Miller. (1999). This book, which offers 60 ideas for graphing with children in grades 1–4, can spur preschool teachers' ideas for creating graphs with younger children.

Math for the very young: A handbook of activities for parents and teachers. Edited by L. Polonsky. (2000). Written by teachers involved with the University of Chicago School Mathematics Project, this guide offers teachers a comprehensive collection of teaching all areas of math to young children.

Children's Books

Derubertis, B. (1999). *A collection for Kate.* New York: Kane Press.

Keena, S., & Girouard, P. (1997). *More or less a mess.* New York: Cartwheel Books.

◇ The Home-School Connection

Hold a Math Night Out, inviting children and their families to learn more about statistics in the early childhood curriculum. Children and their families eat together with teachers and other staff members. The meal could be prepared by the children, who can assemble pizzas during the day and refrigerate them until time to bake them for the meal. Some centers have cooks prepare a meal so families do not have to worry about cooking.

After the meal, introduce families and children to math centers and ask them to circulate among the centers. Equip one table with materials and instructions for the children and families to make a chart using stickers to show how many children and adults are in their families.

Place a second table near a grouping of graphs and charts the children have made during the year to represent their experiences, surveys, and findings from explorations of their world. The children can explain what the charts mean as their family members question them about the graphs.

A third table can revolve around the concepts of most and least. Put sheets of paper containing different numbers of pictures of items on the table. Children and families pick the sheet that has the most items pictured. The table can also have small objects in different baskets. The directions ask the children to make a set of items, and a family member to duplicate the number, adding more or less. Children and family members take turns creating the initial set that each other will follow.

Yet another table can contain photos of the children working and playing in mathematical centers, playing math games, or using math in another way. Children find photos of themselves to place in individual booklets made of a couple pieces of paper stapled between two sheets of construction paper and labeled with each child's name. As they paste the photos in the booklet, children tell their parents about what they were doing and learning, and the parents write this in the book. A teacher stationed at this center may point out to the children that they were represented in the very small photo.

After everyone has had time to visit the centers, teachers explain the mathematical concepts that were utilized in each center. Families and teachers can discuss the mathematic principles children were learning in the center and how these can continue to be fostered in the home.

- When important graphs are constructed, take digital photos of them to e-mail to families. Explain the concept being graphed, how children and teachers constructed the graph, and how to discuss the graph with children.
- Use newsletters to inform parents about children's learning to sort, organize, represent, and analyze data. Let families know that much of young children's learning occurs through spontaneous events. Children learn as they explore their world. But informal learning does not mean unplanned learning. Parents can plan to
- point out circle or bar graphs in grocery or other stores, on signs, or in a newspaper or magazine.
- help children collect and organize things in the home environment. One family expanded on their children's interest in dinosaurs by reading stories of meat- and plant-eating dinosaurs, flying and walking dinosaurs, and so on. They found that their children began sorting dinosaurs into groups by different characteristics.
- provide access to books and ideas that extend children's ideas of mathematics. A book you could recommend is *Family Math* (1986) by Jean Kerr Stanmaker, Virgina Thompson, and Ruth Cossey, published by Equals.

◇ Evaluating and Assessing Children's Learning

The point of collecting and representing information through graphs is to familiarize children with the fact that they can organize and then gain meaning from pictorial descriptions of the things they find through explorations of their world.

Structured Interviews

Structured interviews with individual children can uncover children's thinking about graphs and data organization.

Ask children to sit with you and talk about a familiar graph, chart, or pictorial description of findings. First, ask an open-ended question such as, "What can you tell me about this?" Probe further, asking, "What else do you know about this?" "What do we call this?" Record children's answers.

Then ask each child to point to and talk about specific parts of the graph. Ask the child to point to the *title* and *labels* and tell you what they mean. Children will not read the labels as such, but they should have an idea of what information they convey.

Finish the interview by asking children questions about the meaning of the graph. For example, if the graph depicts the number of children with pets, ask if more children have pets or if more do not; if the graph depicts children's favorite foods, ask which food is the favorite, the next best, and so on. Record findings.

From structured interviews you will be able to gain an understanding of each child's thinking about graphs. This will help you plan the next graphing experience in ways that will match children's existing ideas and extend or clarify them.

Classroom Observations

From time to time scan the room. Note what children are doing, whom they are working with, and how engaged they are. How often do you note children looking at displayed work, graphs, or other posted information? If no children gravitate to charts, graphs, or displays, then it may be that these need to be replaced with fresh charts or graphs. Or if the graphs are new, are they really meaningful to children? Ask yourself how these could be made more meaningful. Could you display them in a place closer to children's activities, use colors that attract the eye, or place them at children's eye level? These observations will give you necessary information that can be used to make graphing experiences more meaningful and useful for the children you teach.

FOR THE CHILDREN

1. Children Will Collect, Organize, and Sort Data

    The ability to collect, organize, and sort data is an important underpinning for algebra and reasoning skills, as well as the foundation for data description and analysis. Children begin early to form groups. First, children pick things from a group of objects on the basis of one characteristic (Copley, 2000): "This is round." Often, however, children just beginning the process of classification can't tell you why they make the sets they do, or will say something like, "They're all like Grandma." Next, children sort entire collections of objects by a single attribute, placing all the round, or red, or fuzzy objects together. At the third level, children sort objects or events on the basis of two or more characteristics: "All of these are round and red." And finally, children can tell you why objects do or do not belong to a given group.

    ◆ Children are natural collectors. They pick up rocks, leaves, seeds, not only just to handle but also to collect. To foster children's collecting, give each child a small plastic bag before going on a walk around the block. One walk could be for children to collect leaves in the bag. Back in the classroom, teachers label each bag with the child's name, then tack the bags to a door frame with the sign "Leaves We Found." Other trips can be taken to collect different colors, sizes, or types of stones, acorns, or pine cones.

    ◆ Create a shelf or corner of the room for play yard supplies. On the shelf include a box of plastic bags, small cardboard boxes to be used for collecting when outside, and a bunch of clear plastic containers for additional collections.

    ◆ To foster children's collecting, ask them why they made the collections they did, or if the objects could be sorted in another way. If children make a collection based on size or shape, ask them how they would sort the objects if each object was the same color.

    ◆ Read *A Collection for Kate* (Derubertis, 1999), a book about children bringing their collections to school. At school the collections are categorized and subcategories counted. You might follow the story and ask children about their collections, or start a class collection.

    ◆ Add sorting boards to the math table. Glue plastic cups on a heavy piece of cardboard or plywood. Make these available for children to use as they sort and count objects. Or boards could be made of heavy cardboard marked into halves or fourths and laminated. Children then use these to sort things in two or four groups. Children could use one side of the board for round things, the other side for things that are not round. Or they could sort by two colors, or any two other variables.

    ◆ Offer children a "junk box." In it, collect all types of things—discarded keys, locks, key chains; large marbles; discarded pens; safety-proofed kitchen tools such as a nutcracker, a small sieve, a tea ball; and

Many everyday experiences, such as how many materials are recycled, can be represented through graphics.

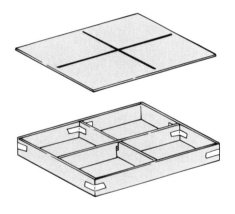

odds and ends from your own junk drawer. Make sure that there aren't duplicates for any of the items. First ask children to play with the junk; then you could ask them to

- find two objects that are the same in some way. One child picked out a plastic fork and a plastic key chain, saying they were the same because they were both made of plastic; another child picked out a brownish acorn and a piece of wood, saying they were the same color.
- pick out a piece of junk that is like a piece you have picked out.
- sort the junk into things that are the same and different. Have children discuss why and how they made their categories. As children do so, record their responses.

Repeat the experience several times during the year. You should see children moving from arbitrary collections to collections based on the attributes of the junk.

2. Children Will Begin to Label Information Collected and Develop an Understanding of Scale

"All these are brown rocks," said 4-year-old Misha, showing his teacher a box of rocks he had collected. "I need a label that says *Brown Rocks*." The teacher asked him to think about how the word *brown* starts, saying, "Listen: *brown,* What letter should I write first?" Misha responded saying, "It's the /b/ sound, but I don't know how to write the rest of it." Together they wrote a label for the box and placed it on the science table.

◆ Let children see you writing labels and titles on charts and graphs.

- As you write, say the word and say each letter.
- Read the labels or titles to the children, and ask them to read these back to you.
- Have children place different labels such as *Our Library* in the places they belong. This way, you'll know children understand a label.

◆ Begin a word wall. When children use a word frequently, place it on the word wall. Before you do so, make certain you follow the previous suggestions. Place words new to the children, or those words they will need to use as they label their own work.

◆ To introduce the idea of scale, take spontaneous photos of children at work and play. When looking over the photos, or making a display using the photos, point out to children how small they look in the photos. Ask them to compare the size of the chair they are sitting on or other piece of furniture in a photo to the actual size of the equipment.

◆ Question how big the toy dinosaurs children play with really were. Ask how much larger a real truck is than the one children are playing with. Point out that the toy house is much smaller than a real house.

3. Children Will Organize Data Through Graphs, Tables, Lists, and So On

To understand graphs, children will need to encounter using tallies or numbers to represent their experience. They need to know that their experiences can be represented in lines or numbers. While using tallies, introduce children to the idea of using columns and rows.

- Use tallies to keep track of how many times a child can jump on one foot and on two feet. Make tallies or use numbers in rows and columns.

    One Foot   Two Feet
    | | | | | | | | | | | | | | | |

Stages in making and understanding graphs have been identified (Charlesworth & Radeloff, 1978). During the first stage of graph making, children use either themselves or real objects to make graphs, but graph only two variables or objects. Next, more than two items are considered, and a more permanent record is constructed. In the third stage of graphing, children can use symbols, such as check marks or squares of paper, to chart their findings.

◆ Construct graphs. First graphs should be as concrete as possible. Often teachers begin graphing experiences using the children themselves to make the graph. Make graphs of children by having them stand in one of two lines to find out

- how many children want to play Looby Loo or Duck, Duck, Goose. Count the children in each line.
- which children eat lunches brought from home and which eat lunches made at school.
- how many children have siblings and how many do not.
- how many boys and girls are in the group.
- which children like vanilla or chocolate pudding.

Be sure to count the children in each group, record the count on a chart, and reach conclusions about how many children were in each line and which line had the most children, the least children, or even no children.

Once children are used to counting themselves and seeing the information being written and then read back to them, begin creating graphs with unit blocks. Tape a child's name to the side of each block. Instead of standing in a line and being counted, each child places his or her block under the correct label. The blocks are counted, and the number in each stack recorded and discussed. Use the blocks to chart and record

- the number of children in school
- children who have pets and those who do not
- children wearing something red and those who are not wearing anything red
- children who like peanut butter and those who do not

A group of 3-year-olds graphed their height, building with cardboard blocks to equal their height. The blocks were stacked in a row, and each child stood by his or her stack of blocks.

◆ Make floor graphs. Children can construct graphs using poster boards, a piece of flannel, or large construction paper placed on the floor. They can place small pictures, cutouts, and small photos of themselves; plastic/wooden animals, people, buildings, and cars; or other objects and items in rows to make graphs of

- farm and zoo animals, animals they know, and those they've never seen
- clothes they wear and those they do not wear
- cars they like and those they do not
- yes or no answers to the questions "Do you have . . . ?" "Do you like . . . ?" "Have you been to . . . ?" "Do you enjoy . . . ?"

◆ Use cash register tape for graphs.
- Measure the height of a bean plant each day and record each day's growth on a piece of register tape.
- Chart and record each child's height and weight using cash register tape.
- Use register tape to chart and record the number of inches of rain that falls in a given week.
- Chart and record the height of block buildings using register tape.

◆ Moving from the concrete to the abstract, you can construct graphs using paper and markers, pictures, colored paper squares, blocks, and other materials.
- Ask children to count the number of birds they see at the bird feeder. You might find bird pictures or stickers of birds common to the area and use these to make a pictorial graph of "Birds at the Feeder."
- Observe the number of cars passing by the center during a given time. Count the cars or trucks, and using pictures or stickers of vehicles, record your findings.

◆ First graphing experiences continue moving from the concrete to the abstract, and involve only two categories.

Make a graphing tray. Like the sorting tray, glue small plastic glasses to heavy cardboard or plywood. Make two rows of glasses. Provide children with small objects to sort to create a graph. You might give them a box of two types of animals (farm and zoo), a box of small cars and trucks, or a box of small plastic people and children. The point is to fill the two rows of cups with the different objects to create a graph. Then children count the number of objects in each category.

◆ All graphing activities should stem from something of high interest to children. Teachers who base the curriculum on the resources found in the children's environment will find plenty of interesting things for children to graph.

- A group of 3-year-olds studied babies. In the process they sang baby lullabies. Feeling very grown-up and independent because they were now big enough to sing lullabies to babies, they made a graph of their favorite lullabies.

- Another group studied musical instruments. One of the mothers came to the class and played a violin. Children were taught to pick out a melody on the piano, and they listened to their favorite songs played on the violin and piano. To reach closure, the children graphed which music they liked best, violin or piano. The children asked the teacher for a third category, *Both Violin and Piano,* because they "liked both of them." To make this graph, children colored in a square under the appropriate label.

- Children visiting a farm were impressed when the farmer said she measured her horse with her hands. Her horse was 16 hands high. Back in the classroom children measured things in their room with their hands and made a graph of cut-out hands.

- Children studying themselves created graphs of eye and hair color.

- One group of 5-year-olds made a graph of clothes they would like to wear if they were teenagers and clothes they had to wear now.

   Continuing the study of clothing, children made graphs to represent the different ways their shoes closed. The graph titled "Shoes" included categories for *Tie Shoes, Velcro, Slip-Ons,* and *Buckle Shoes.*

- Children who had visited a shoe store were given a foot measure to use in their classroom. The 3-year-olds enjoyed measuring their feet with and without shoes. After the play waned, the teacher asked them to measure their shoes. The lengths of children's shoes were recorded on a graph, and the children decided that most of them wore the same size shoes.

- One teacher of 4-year-olds introduced children to concepts of story structure and genre. Often after reading a book, she would ask children who their favorite characters were. After reading several folktales—*Three Little Pigs, Little Red Riding Hood, Three Billy Goats Gruff*—she asked children to talk about their favorite characters in the stories. Using the three tales, children listed their favorite characters. Then they talked about the villains in the stories and listed their favorite villains.

   Another week, the teacher read a group of current stories. She then asked children to vote for their favorite current story and their favorite folktale. Recording their votes in a graph, the children compared stories they liked.

- When children studied the way their clothing was closed, they noted that some items were held together with ties, other items with zippers, buttons, or Velcro. A chart was made titled "Our Clothing," with the categories *Ties, Buttons, Zippers,* and *Velcro.*

    Finally, the children counted just the number of buttons on the coats they wore to play outside when it was cold and graphed their findings. They found that the majority of children had six buttons on their coats. The experiences of counting and graphing buttons—and shoe sizes, clothing, and so forth—serve as foundational knowledge for the learning of the meaning of *mode,* which will come later in children's lives.

- A group of 4-year-olds was planting a garden. The teacher provided eight packets of different types of flower seeds. Children chose a partner and then the pack of seeds they wanted to plant. Pasted along one side of a piece of cardboard, the empty seed packets were used to construct a graph. In the next spaces, children wrote their names. The remaining spaces were used to chart when which seeds started sprouting, how fast they grew within a week, and when the first flower appeared, giving children and visitors to the room a great deal of information about the children's experiences.

- Number charts can be made of favorite finger plays. Using five or ten *Little Chickadees, Frogs, Monkeys Jumping on a Bed, Pumpkins,* or *Birds,* teachers and children can create a number chart.

- Votes need a way of being recorded. Children's preferences for any number of things or events can be recorded in a graph.

◆ Introduce children to pie graphs. Pie graphs can be constructed from paper circles, paper plates, or tinfoil pans. The point is to divide the circle space in ways that represent children's ideas or specific categories. A pie graph might be used to illustrate children's

- favorite colors
- best-liked foods
- favorite drinks

◆ Ask children to conduct surveys and chart the results in graph form.

- One group of 5-year-olds questioned why there was so much trash around their building. They decided it was the adults who were leaving the trash, not the children—obviously they would never throw paper on their school grounds! In teams, the children interviewed the directors, teachers, and other center staff. Then when parents came to pick up their children, the same teams interviewed different parents. The children told the people that they were concerned that there was too much trash around the building. The question they asked the adults was, "Why do you think there's trash around our school?"

    The responses were graphed. Adults responded that people were careless, thoughtless, or in a hurry. Most of the adults, however, said that there were no trash bins near or around the school. The children then proposed to the parent board that trash bins be provided in areas around the school. The delight of the children when their mission was achieved and the pride they felt when they were able to solve a real problem were immense.

- Another group surveyed adults working in the school to find out what their favorite foods were. The children also interviewed family members. With the teacher's help, children charted the favorite foods of adults. They then compared the adults' favorite foods to their own and made another graph that illustrated foods both adults and children liked.

4. Children Will Gain Meaning from Graphs, Tables, Lists, and so on

"What is this?" a visiting supervisor asked 3-year-old children as she pointed to a graph on the wall. "We ate baby cereal," said one child. Another chimed in, "And we ate our cereal." A third child, pointing to the graph with all the names listed under "Our Cereal," and none under the label "Baby Cereal," said, "Nobody likes baby cereal, NOBODY." Then they all chimed in, "Baby cereal is yucky, yucky, yucky, yucky!"

The supervisor complimented the teacher, saying, "You know, I'm used to seeing graphs in preschools and asking children what they mean. And I'm also used to children saying "I don't know," which tells me the teacher made the graph with no input from the children. Your children, because they actually participated in preparing the graph, knew exactly what it meant."

While it is easy for teachers to make graphs, it is not easy for young children to understand graphs. Graphs incorporate a number of number skills and understandings. To understand graphs, children need some idea of

- one-to-one correspondence
- counting
- comparing more or less
- numbers and their names
- the difference between horizontal and vertical

◆ As the teacher of the 3-year-olds did with the cereal, you can make graphs meaningful for children of any age.

- Make sure graphing stems from a real experience.
- Read the graph with individual children and ask

Which has the most?	Which is longest?
Which has the least?	What is the same as?
Is there more or less?	What do some of the children like?
What is heavier/lighter?	Which are rough/smooth?

- Use words such as *none, all, some, most, a lot, longest, tallest, shortest,* and so on to describe the data.
- Refer to the information on the graph: "We voted for . . . ," or "Remember, most of the children wanted to . . . ." In addition to questioning, discuss the problem or the reason children made the graph and talk about what the graph means.
- Make the home-school connection by sending copies of graphs to parents with explanations of what the children did and what their graphs mean.

◇ Reflecting

In a way, creating and reading graphs give children a way to reflect and think about their experiences. By organizing information, graphs inform children of trends as well as central tendency.

Obviously it will be a long time before children need to understand trends and central tendency (mean and mode). Regardless, graphs introduce children to these concepts.

As children read graphs, ask them to reach conclusions: "What is our favorite story?" "What games do we like the best?" "Why do you think no one voted for baby cereal?"

◇ Extending and Expanding to the Primary Grades

Graphing that begins during the early years lays the foundation for more complicated graphing in the primary grades. In the primary grades, children can

- construct their own graphs using any number of variables represented by numbers displayed in columns and rows.
- begin developing ideas of central tendency, finding the mean and mode on graphs.
- start thinking about probability. They might shake two color chips in a shaker and then graph, perhaps using toothpicks or tallies, the number of times each color comes up. Using 10 counters, children can next count the number of times the blue sides were up and the red sides were up, practicing addition.
- graph week- or month-long events, charting/graphing which month has the most birthdays, what time children go to bed and wake up, or how many holidays there are in each month or the entire year.
- use larger numbers. They might graph how many pieces of popcorn different cups or containers can hold or how many kernels in bags of different brands of popcorn are found after popping, or they could guess how many of pieces of popcorn are on a paper plate, charting their names, guesses, and the exact popcorn count.

◇ Documenting Children's Learning

This Web documents some of the important mathematical learning and content from other disciplines children gain while exploring the ideas of data description, organization, representation, and analysis.

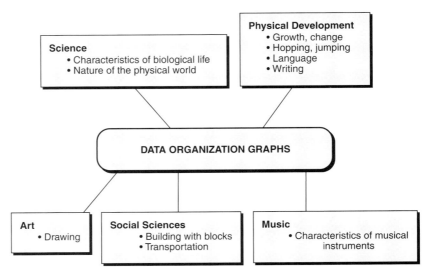

EXPERIENCE 6

Math Problem Solving

FOR THE TEACHER

◇ What You'll Need to Know

Young children, filled with curiosity, are natural problem solvers. They come into this world wired for learning. From the moment of birth, children begin the process of observing, looking, and listening. In an attempt to make sense of the world in which they find themselves, children actively explore their world. They feel, put things in their mouth, take things apart, pull, push, tear, pick up, and drop things—all to try to find out more about the nature of the things in their world.

Within the context of a high quality early childhood classroom, children have time, freedom, and opportunity to extend and expand their natural problem-solving skills. Their explorations become more directed and purposeful in good schools for young children. Children learn to ask questions, collect data, reflect, and solve real problems. As they do so, they develop the ability to identify and solve problems coming from daily life, as well as develop number and other mathematical knowledge and skills.

It seems as if there is no need to foster children's ability to question. By age 3, children seem to ask way too many questions: "What's dis? Dat?" "How much money do you have?" "Why is there more here?" These first questions are sometimes asked to express wonder and surprise with the world (Piaget & Inhelder, 1969). Four- and five-year-olds continue to ask "Why?" They, however, often really do want to know *why*: "Why are there three ducks?" And they ask "Why?" because they really want to know causal relations: "Why is it heavy?" "Why does she have more?"

In the preschool, children's questions are respected. But teachers do more than respect questions. They model asking questions: "How many more do you need?" "What could you do here?" "What will happen if. . . ?" And then they deliberately arrange the environment to bring children face-to-face with asking real questions themselves.

Problem solving, which begins with asking questions, involves the skills of observing. Again, children come to school with fully developed observational skills. They've looked, mouthed, torn apart, dropped, and spilled things in an attempt to find out more about their world. In the preschool, however, teachers focus children's attention on using their senses. Sometimes, teachers may ask children to focus on using one sense at a time, to really look, listen, or feel and touch. At other times, children might be asked to use all of their senses at once, to look, look again, listen, touch, or handle and feel.

Once children observe, there must be some way for them to organize their findings through collections, displays, graphs, or other methods described in Experience 5. The final stage of problem solving involves children reflecting and thinking about their findings and then reaching conclusions.

Mathematical problem solving is central to learning mathematics. It's through problem solving—sensing a problem, posing questions, observing and collecting information, organizing the information, and reaching conclusions—that children have opportunities to apply their mathematical knowledge and skills. Whether children are asking questions, observing, finding out, or reaching conclusions, they will need to apply their knowledge and skills of counting, number operations, graphing, measuring, working with shapes, or beginning concepts of algebra.

◇ Key Concepts

- Problem solving begins by sensing a problem and posing thoughtful questions.
- All the senses are used to collect information about the problem to be solved. Vicarious information, books, CDs, and Web information can be used to extend and expand children's firsthand experiences.

- Information or data must be collected and organized in some representational way.
- Information collected—the data—is analyzed. The processes of reflection and reaching conclusions constitute the final stage of problem solving.
- The problem-solving processes are intimately involved in all areas of mathematics: knowledge of numbers, counting, measuring, graphing, beginning algebra, and geometry.

◇ Goals and Objectives

Mathematical problem solving means children will use mathematic concepts and skills to engage in a task for which the solution is not clearly known. This means children will use the knowledge they have and the processes of problem solving to develop new mathematical understandings.

Applying counting, algebra, geometry, measuring, and data organization to solving problems, the following goals and objectives will be achieved:

Children will develop the ability to sense problems by asking thoughtful questions.

Children, using mathematical concepts, will increase their observational skills.

Children will begin to organize information in representational ways.

Children will analyze data, reaching conclusions.

◇ What You'll Need

A copy of the National Council of Teachers of Mathematics Standard 3 will be useful to teachers (*http://standards.Nctm.org/document/chapter3/prob.htm*).

Let's Do Math (*http://www.gov/pubs/parents/LearnPtnrs/math.html*)

Children's Books

Anno, M. (1999). *Anno's magic seeds.* New York: Paper Star.

Burns, M. (1996). *How many feet? How many tails?* New York: Scholastic Trade.

Keenan, S. (2001). *Lizzy's dizzy day, dizzy day.* New York: Cartwheel Books.

◇ The Home-School Connection

Mathematical problem solving should take place at home and in the preschool. To involve children's families in mathematical problem-solving activities, you might do the following:

- Obtain a copy of *Let's Do Math.* The ideas in this Web resource have been revised in Tear-out Sheet 1 at the end of this experience to match the mathematical abilities of children ages 3-5. Put this on your Web page, or duplicate it and send it home to families.
- During a parent meeting, show photos of children solving mathematical problems. Ask parents to brainstorm the types of math problems their children could solve at home.

◇ Evaluating and Assessing Children's Learning

Differing forms of observing can be employed to evaluate and assess young children's development of problem-solving skills.

- Label 3" × 5" cards with children's names. Pick three or four of these each day. During the day, observe these children during work and play time. Record any time they ask a question. Note the type of question and whether they waited for a response or tried to answer the question themselves or with others. You should see children moving

    - from asking questions in wonder, "Why is the sky blue?" to questions with a purpose, "How can these fit?"

    - from asking questions, but not waiting for a response, to waiting for a response.

    - from not noticing mathematical problems to identifying mathematical problems and using strategies of working backward, counting on their fingers, or counting objects to try to answer questions on their own.

- Plan a structured interview and observe each child solving a mathematical problem. You might

    - present children with a set of objects and ask them to add the number of items it would take to make a given number. Ask children how they solved the problem, and record the strategies they used.

    - give children problems to solve. Using small toys, ask them how they would share four cars with six children, or what they would do if they had eight cookies and four children. When they respond, ask them why they reached that conclusion, and record the strategies they used.

FOR THE CHILDREN

Mathematical problem solving should be an integral part of children's daily lives. Good mathematical problems can be embedded in any type of meaningful experience and topic of interest to the children. In this way, problem-solving skills and abilities integrate the curriculum.

◇ Project Work

The premise of this book is that children learn best when their minds and bodies are actively engaged in meaningful experiences. Project, thematic, or unit work offers children the best opportunity to do so. Whatever the theme or topic, you can integrate the significant mathematical problem-solving processes and skills of questioning, observing, comparing, and contrasting. Throughout, children will experience

- understanding that there is a problem
- planning how to solve it
- carrying out the plan
- reviewing the solution

Experience 6 ◆ Math Problem Solving

> ## MODELING QUESTIONING SKILLS
>
> Every day teachers model questioning. They frequently ask children questions such as, How many cups will it take to fill this bucket? Why is this nut and bolt heavier than this larger acorn? Who is tallest? Who has the longest piece of yarn? How many times can you jump? How far can you jump? Which of these is heaviest? Which is smallest?
>
> Because teachers want children to develop mathematical problem-solving strategies, they should frequently ask children about the strategies they used to solve problems.
>
> - Do you have a plan?
> - How did you get that answer? Is there another way to find out?
> - Why do you think that is true?
> - What are you thinking of?
> - Are you finding an answer? Have you tried thinking another way?
> - Are you sure?
> - What would happen if . . . ?
> - Why?

1. Children Will Gain Skills in Asking Mathematical Questions

   Project work begins with a question or problem to be solved. The question can come from the teacher who observes, listens to, and questions children to determine their interests, or from a child or group of children.

   Babies, the theme of a group of 3- and 4-year-olds, was precipitated by the children. Several of the children had new babies in their families. Other children showed interest in the idea of a new baby in a family. Many made disparaging comments: "Babies poop in their pants. It's uky, iky, poopy." "They're dumb. Babies can't even eat—they spit food all over. It's all icky."

   Picking up on the children's interest in babies, the teacher asked the children what they knew about babies, and what they would like to know. She recorded their responses on a chart and reviewed these with the children. She noted that none of the children asked any questions involving mathematical concepts, and she planned to add math questions and concepts as they studied babies.

   One of the families brought a baby to the center. As the children held the baby, observed her nursing, and watched her playing, they began to ask questions.

   One, holding the baby, said, "She's heavy. She must weigh a ton. How much does she weigh?" The child's questioning demonstrated children's ability to sense a problem and ask questions. The teacher asked how they could find out if babies were really heavy. The children, used to being asked to solve problems, said you could find out how heavy babies were. One said, "You could look

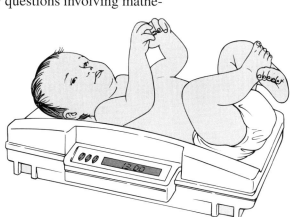

at the baby, and maybe see if it was really big or really little." Another said, "No, you weigh babies. That's what you do." The next day another mother brought her baby and a baby scale to the center. The children watched as the baby was weighed. The teacher recorded the baby's weight, 13 pounds, on a chart. Then the children weighed themselves. The teacher charted their weights as well. Even though these very young children were just beginning to develop concepts of greater than and less than, they were impressed at how much more they weighed than the baby. "We're bigger, really bigger," they said, illustrating that they had initial ideas of how to answer a question and reach conclusions.

Next the teacher informed the children that they too had been babies. She gave them "homework"—to answer the question "How much did you weigh when you were born?" Once the children knew their birth weights, they and the teacher took shovels and a scale to the sand pile. With the aid of several helpers, each child filled a plastic bag with sand until it equaled his or her birth weight. They carried the bags around and reached conclusions. "I was this big," said one child lifting her bag of sand. Another said, "This is heavy! I was heavy, heavy, heavy."

The children, picking up on the teacher's questions, began to ask other questions:

> Look, my hand is bigger than a baby's hand—how big is my hand?
>
> How much longer are my feet than the baby's feet?
>
> How much bigger am I than the baby?

As the goal is to have children pose thoughtful, mathematical questions, the teacher observed children during work and play. She noted which children were asking questions involving mathematical concepts in order to solve problems they were facing. She found that children were moving from just asking "Why?" to asking "How many . . . ?" "How much . . . ?" as well as purposeful "Why?" questions—"Why is this heavy?" "Why doesn't this fit?"

2. Children Will Gain Skills in Predicting Mathematical Outcomes

In the group using the theme of babies, the teacher encouraged the children to make predictions:

- How much weight will a baby gain in a month? How much will you gain?
- How many spoonfuls of baby cereal will the baby eat?
- How many spoonfuls of cereal do you eat?
- How many children in the group have baby brothers? Baby sisters? Older brothers? Older sisters?

The teacher recorded children's predictions, and together the children and teacher discussed these, made comparisons, and reached conclusions.

◆ You do not need a baby for children to make predictions. They can make many predictions while playing with water and sand.

- Use water play as an opportunity to make predictions. Add soap or any substance to make strong bubbles in the water. Ask children to predict how many bubbles they can make using just their hands. What shape will the bubbles be? Add other equipment to the water such as plastic bottles, spoons, hoops, and other objects that have the potential to be bubble-making machines. Ask children to predict if an object can be used to make bubbles or not, and how many bubbles it will make. Have children count the bubbles and sketch their findings.

- Use sand play as an opportunity to make predictions. Ask children how they could make sand stick together so they could actually build with it. Then they could predict what will happen to the sand buildings constructed with the use of water after they sit in the sun.

Of course, children can predict and count how many cups of sand will fit in a given container, if a sieve will hold sand, and what will happen to the sand if they use it to fill a pipe.

Continue prediction activities. Children can predict

- how many days before it will rain again
- whose corn seed will sprout first
- how many insects they will find under a rock
- how far the windup toy will go
- how many tomatoes will grow on their tomato plant
- how many apples will fit in a basket
- how much the pumpkin weighs

3. Children Will Gain Skills in Observing

Children can be astute observers. In good schools for young children, natural observing skills are expanded and extended. The process of refining children's observation skills includes observing number and other mathematic concepts.

Still studying babies, the teacher asked children to move around the room. She encouraged them to move every body part they could, and listed the parts as children solved the problem of moving everything they could. They listed feet, hands, head, legs, trunk, and arms. Then when another baby was brought to the classroom, the children asked, "How does the baby move?" Stating, "Babies can't walk. But what can they do?" the teacher asked the children to observe a baby just learning to crawl, and to count and then list all the body parts the baby moved. Observing children counted eyes, fingers, hands, arms, feet, legs, and head.

◆ Moving beyond the observation of babies, ask children to observe the number of different kinds of plants growing in a given spot. You might give children a hula hoop or a circle of string to place on the ground, and have them observe and count the plants inside it. Or they could count any insect life they find.

◆ Observe insects. Really look at them. How many wings, eyes, and legs do they have? Now ask children to really look at spiders. How many eyes, wings, and legs do they have? Have children count and reach conclusions about how spiders and insects are alike and different. Have them sketch their findings.

Everyday experiences abound with opportunities for children to solve problems.

- As children observe insects, introduce the idea of symmetry. Using a specimen, place a file card over one half of the insect. Ask children to predict what the covered side looks like. If they have observed insects carefully and thoughtfully, they'll tell you it's just like the side they can see. Purchase ladybugs from a science supply shop and observe how symmetrical they are.

- Find and bring a caterpillar to the group. Place it on a piece of clear plastic and ask children to really look at it. How many eyes does the caterpillar have? How many legs? Are any of the parts symmetrical? Hold the plastic above the children and ask them to observe how the caterpillar moves. How many legs move at a time?

4. Children Will Gain Skills in Comparing and Contrasting

Being able to make comparisons means that children are able to find a relationship between two or more sets of things on the basis of specific attributes or characteristics. For example, the children's work revolving around the theme of babies involved a great deal of comparing and contrasting on the attributes of weight, length, movement, and other characteristics.

In addition to comparing and contrasting experiences during project work, you can arrange for children to compare and contrast numbers. Some of these opportunities can be structured; other opportunities to compare and contrast are a part of children's living and occur spontaneously.

- Use structured experiences.
    - Make sets of baby cards. Use a rubber stamp of a baby or stickers, and heavy laminated paper cards. Make two cards with one baby on each card, two cards with two babies on each, and so on, to ten babies. Vary the arrangement of babies on each card. Children then sort the cards by those that depict the same number of babies.
    - Show children a card and have them find another one that has one more, two more, or three more babies on it.

Experience 6 ◆ Math Problem Solving

- Show children a set of objects and ask them to create a set that has the same number.
- Show sets of objects or cards that depict differing numbers. Ask children which set has more.
- Use the counting materials at the math table for comparing and contrasting by making sets of light, heavy, fuzzy, rough, and smooth things.
- Use flannel boards and flannel or Velcro-backed cutouts that children can arrange in sets that are equal in number and sets that are not. You might provide children with pictures of farm animals, vehicles, hats and heads, dolls and doll clothes, or dinosaurs.

As children arrange sets, remind them to count the number of objects in a set so they can find out which set has more, has less, is equal to, or is not equal to.

◆ Use spontaneous experiences. During daily living there will be many opportunities for children to make comparisons on the basis of number concepts.

- When two children are painting at easels, you might ask them to count and compare the number of colors used in each of their paintings.
- One classroom bought ladybugs for their garden. After the insects were released, the children counted the ladybugs each saw and recorded their counts. Then they compared how many ladybugs they each saw in their garden the next day.
- "He has more cookies," complains Tonja. When this happens, count and compare how many cookies, blocks, puzzle pieces, dolls, or books children have at a given time.
- "I can make a longer snake than you," says Antonio, working at the clay table rolling and rolling a snake. The other children can join in comparing who made the longest snake and the shortest.

5. Children Will Gain Skills in Reflecting

Children can represent their problem-solving strategies through drawings, paintings, or construction. Drawing, painting, or representing their math work in some other concrete way forces children to think, rethink, evaluate, and reflect on their work.

The children studying babies, drew babies. Because they had actually experienced a baby and had taken turns holding one, their drawings were highly representational. The pictures demonstrated that drawing is a cognitive activity—the more children knew about babies, the greater their ability to symbolically represent babies with markers and paper.

◆ Start keeping math journals. You might start by making a big math journal for the group. In the journal, keep important dates, announce the two new puzzles at the math table, record how many moths emerged from the cocoons or how many eggs hatched, or record each child's birthday complete with a picture of a birthday cake that the child finishes by drawing the exact number of candles that represent his or her age.

Children in kindergarten can begin to keep their own math journals. They can

- record math ideas they know
- draw how they solved a math problem
- keep important dates
- record numbers and number operations meaningful to them

◆ Make math murals.

- Use a familiar counting rhyme such as *Five Little Speckled Frogs* (or ten if the children are ready for a longer sequence). On a piece of large mural paper, label the sides from one to five. Children then fill in the picture of the correct number of frogs eating their lunches on a log. Do the same with *Ten in the Bed, Ten Little Babies Bouncing on the Bed,* or any other counting rhyme or book.
- Make murals of children's growth and development. Divide a sheet of mural paper into two sections. Label the sections *When I Was a Baby* and *Now I'm Big*. Children record their weight as a baby and their current weight and draw pictures of themselves.

6. Children Will Reach Conclusions

The final step in problem solving is to reach conclusions. Throughout the study of babies, children made many conclusions. The group brainstormed and told all the things they now knew about babies. These were listed on a chart. The children then made their own book of babies, dictating and using invented spelling and pictures to portray the conclusions they reached about babies.

◇ Extending and Expanding to the Primary Grades

Children in the primary grades would be attracted to *Journey North,* a global study of migration at *http:www.learner/org/north/*. As they study a migrating species—whales or monarch butterflies—or when emperor tulips bloom, children will apply every mathematic skill and concept and fulfill every standard of the National Council of Teachers of Mathematics.

◇ Documenting Children's Learning

Reflect on the math concepts and skills the children utilized as they implemented a project by creating a Web.

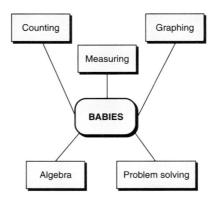

Tear-Out Sheet 1

Let's Do Math

You use math to solve problems every day. Involve your children in these daily problem-solving experiences.

Go grocery shopping. Even toddlers can help you grocery shop.

- Before you shop, read the grocery sales page of the paper with your children. Ask them to select an item or two from the pages that they want to purchase. Talk about how much the items cost, and include the items on your grocery list.
- As you shop at the store, remind your children to shop for the items they've selected.
- Ask children to guess the number of apples that equal 2 pounds. Help them select as many apples as are needed for the desired weight.
- Find two cans of tomato soup.

Let the children see you paying for the groceries. If you use checks or credit cards, make sure children know that these are like money. When you're back from the store, children can

- help you put groceries away, putting a box of rice on the bottom shelf, the bag of pretzels on the second shelf, and so on.
- count the number of fruits, vegetables, cans, or jars you've purchased.
- decide if there's more fruit or vegetables, more bread or butter, more canned or jarred goods.
- pick one snack item to eat.

Show you enjoy numbers.

- Play number games with children, from *This Little Piggy* to bingo, card games, and board games.
- Let children see you solve problems by counting, adding, or subtracting: "I need two more cups." "Help me button the last one." "How many more do I need?" "I have too many. What should I do?"

Use toys to teach problem solving and number concepts.

- Balls
  - Which ball is the largest? The smallest?
  - How many times did you catch the ball?
  - How many balls do we have here?
  - How far can you toss each ball? How would you know?
  - Which balls float? Let's try them in this bucket of water.
  - How do balls behave when rolled on the grass, ground, and sidewalk?

Permission is granted by the publisher to reproduce these pages.

- Blocks
    - How tall can you build?
    - How many circle blocks are there?
    - How many blocks are in your building?
    - Make a house big enough for your car/doll/teddy bear.
- Boxes
    - Which box is the largest?
    - How many boxes can you stack before they fall?
    - How many smaller boxes fit inside the larger box?

Share household chores.

- Sort laundry. Even the youngest children can help with the laundry. Have them sort and pile clothes from the dryer and take them to the places they belong. Children can sort their own clothes and take them to their rooms, as well as clothes belonging to other members of the family.
- Set the table. By setting the table, children are gaining experience in using one-to-one correspondence—one napkin, one fork, etc., at each place.
- Select clothes. When selecting their own clothes to wear the next day, children are thinking ahead, matching socks to shoes and to feet, and again gaining skills in one-to-one correspondence.

References

Alexander, K. L., & Entwisle, D. R. (1988). Achievement in the first 2 years of school: Patterns and processes. *Monographs of the Society for Research in Child Development, 53* (2, Serial No. 288).

Andrews, A. G., & Trafton, P. R. (2002). *Little kids, powerful problem solvers: Math stories from a kindergarten classroom.* Portsmouth, NH: Heinemann.

Barbour, N., & Seefeldt, C. (1993). *Developmental continuity across preschool and primary grades.* Olney, MD: Association for Childhood Education International.

Baroody, A. J., & Wilkins, J. L. M. (1999). The development of informal counting, number, and arithmetic skills and concepts in the primary grades. In J. V. Copley (Ed.), *Mathematics in the early years* (pp. 48–65). Reston, VA: National Council of Teachers of Mathematics; Washington, DC: National Association for the Education of Young Children.

Basile, C. (1999). The outdoors as a context for mathematics in the early years. In J. V. Copley (Ed.), *Mathematics in the early years* (pp. 150–161). Reston, VA: National Council of Teachers of Mathematics; Washington, DC: National Association for the Education of Young Children.

Berk, L. E., & Winsler, A. (1995). *Scaffolding children's learning: Vygotsky and early childhood education.* Washington, DC: National Association for the Education of Young Children.

Blaska, J. K., & Lynch, E. C. (1998). Is everyone included: Using children's literature to facilitate the understanding of disabilities. *Young Children, 53*(2) 36–40.

Bredekamp, S. (1993, November). Reflections on Reggio Emilia. *Young Children,* p. 13.

Bredekamp, S. (1998). *Tools for teaching developmentally appropriate practice—The leading edge in early childhood education.* Washington, DC: National Association for the Education of Young Children.

Bredekamp, S., & Copple, C. (1997). *Developmentally appropriate practices in early childhood programs* (rev. ed.). Washington, DC: National Association for the Education of young children.

Bredekamp, S., & Rosegrant, T. (1995). *Reaching potentials: Transforming early childhood curriculum and assessment* (Vol. 2). Washington, DC: National Association for the Education of Young Children.

Bronfenbrenner, U. (1979). *The ecology of human development: Experiments by nature and design.* Cambridge, MA: Harvard University Press.

Bronson, M. B. (1995). *The right stuff for children birth to 8: Selecting play materials to support development.* Washington, DC: National Association for the Education of Young Children.

Bruner, J. (1966). *Toward a theory of instruction.* Cambridge, MA: Belknap/Harvard.

Burns, M. (1993). *Math and literature (k–3).* Sausalito, CA: Marilyn Burns Education Associates.

Charlesworth, R. (2000). *Experiences in math for young children.* Albany, NY: Delmar.

Charlesworth, R., Hart, C. H., Burts, D. C., & DeWolf, M. (1993). The LSU studies: Building a research base for developmentally appropriate practice. In S. Reifel (Ed.), *Perspectives on developmentally appropriate practice: Vol. 5. Advances in early education and day care* (pp. 3–28). Greenwich, CT: JAI Press.

Charlesworth, R., & Radeloff, D. J. (1978). *Experiences in math for young children.* Albany, NY: Delmar.

Clements, D. H. (1999). The effective use of computers with young children. In J. V. Copley (Ed.), *Mathematics in the early years* (pp. 119–128). Reston, VA: National Council of Teachers of Mathematics; Washington, DC: National Association for the Education of Young Children.

Clements, D. H. (1999). Geometric and spatial thinking in young children. In J. V. Copley (Ed.), *Mathematics in the early years* (pp. 66–79). Reston, VA: National Council of Teachers of Mathematics; Washington, DC: National Association for the Education of Young Children.

Commune di Reggio Emilia. (1987). *To make a portrait of a lion.* Reggio Emilia, Italy: Author.

Copley, J. V. (2000). *The young child and mathematics.* Reston, VA: National Council of Teachers of Mathematics; Washington, DC: National Association for the Education of Young Children.

Davila Coates, G., & Thompson, V. (1999). Involving parents of four- and five-year-olds in their children's mathematics education: The FAMILY MATH experience. In J. V. Copley (Ed.), *Mathematics in the early years* (pp. 198–214). Reston, VA: National Council of Teachers of Mathematics.

Dewey, J. (1938). *Experience and education.* New York: Collier Books.

Dewey, J. (1944). *Democracy and education.* New York: The Free Press.

Dighe, J., Calomiris, Z., & Van Zutphen, C. (1998). Nurturing the language of art in children. *Young Children, 53*(1), 4–9.

Dyson, A. H. (1988). The value of time off-task—Young children's spontaneous talk and deliberate text. *Harvard Educational Review, 97,* 396–420.

Findell, C. R., Small, M., Cavanagh, M., Dacey, L., Greenes, C. E., & Shellfield, L. J. (2001). *Navigating through geometry in prekindergarten–grade 2 (with CD-Rom).* Reston, VA: National Council of Teachers of Mathematics.

Flynn, L. L., & Kieff, J. (2002). Including everyone in outdoor play. *Young Children, 57*(3), 20–26.

Galper, A., Wigfield, A., & Seefeldt, C. (1997). Head Start parents' beliefs about their children's abilities, task values, and performances on different activities. *Child Development, 68,* 897–908.

Geist, E. (2001). Children are born mathematicians: Promoting the construction of early mathematical concepts in children under five. *Young Children, 56*(4), 12–19.

Gesell, A., Ilg, F. L., & Ames, L. B. (1974). *Infant and child in the culture of today.* New York: Harper & Row.

Greenes, C. (1999). The Boston University—Chelsea Project. In J. V. Copley (Ed.), *Mathematics in the early years* (pp. 151–155). Reston, VA: National Council of Teachers of Mathematics; Washington, DC: National Association for the Education of Young Children.

Greenes, C. (1999). Ready to learn: Developing young children's mathematical powers. In J. V. Copley (Ed.), *Mathematics in the early years* (pp. 39–47). Reston, VA: National Council of Teachers of Mathematics; Washington, DC: National Association for the Education of Young Children.

Johnson-Foote, B. (2001). *Cup cooking.* Beltsville, MD: Gryphon House.

Katz, L. (1993). What can we learn from Reggio Emilia? In C. Edwards, L. Gandini, & G. Forman (Eds.), *The hundred languages of children* (pp. 19–41). Norwood, NJ: Ablex.

Katz, L. (1998). *The leading edge.* Washington, DC: National Association for the Education of Young Children.

Kim, S. L. (1999). Teaching mathematics through musical activities. In J. V. Copley (Ed.), *Mathematics in the early years* (pp. 146–150). Reston, VA: National Council of Teachers of Mathematics; Washington, DC: National Association for the Education of Young Children.

References

Loughlin, C., & Suina, J. (1982). *The learning environment: An instructional strategy.* New York: Teachers College Press.

Mallory, B. L. (1998). Educating young children with developmental differences: Principles of inclusive practice. In C. Seefeldt & A. Galper (Eds.), *Continuing issues in early childhood education* (2nd ed., p. 228). Upper Saddle River, NJ: Merrill/Prentice Hall.

Mallory, B. L., & New, R. S. (1994). *Diversity & developmentally appropriate practices: Challenges to early childhood education.* New York: Teachers College Press.

Marcon, R. (1992). Differential effects of three preschool models on inner-city 4-year olds. *Early Childhood Research Quarterly, 7,* 517–530.

Martin, L., & Miller, M. (1999). *Great graphing.* New York: Scholastic.

Maryland State Department of Education. (1992). *Laying the foundation for the future.* Baltimore, MD: Author.

Marzoff, D. P., & DeLoache, J. S. (1994). Transfer in young children's understanding of spatial representations. *Child Development, 29,* 739–752.

McCracken, J. (1990). *More than 1, 2, 3: The real basics of mathematics.* Washington, DC: National Association for the Education of Young Children.

National Council of Teachers of Mathematics. (1975). *Mathematics learning in early childhood.* Reston, VA: Author.

National Council of Teachers of Mathematics (1989). *Curriculum and evaluation standards for school mathematics.* Reston, VA: Author.

National Council of Teachers of Mathematics. (2000). *Principles and standards for school mathematics.* Reston, VA: Author.

National Council of Teachers of Mathematics and the National Association for the Education of Young Children. (2002). *Early childhood mathematics: Promoting good beginnings.* Reston, VA: Author; Washington, DC: Author.

National Council of Teachers of Mathematics and the National Association for the Education of Young Children. (2002). *Learning paths and teaching strategies in early mathematics.* Reston, VA: Author.

National Research Council. (1996). *National science education standards.* Washington, DC: National Academy Press.

National Research Council. (2001). *Adding it up: Helping children learn mathematics.* J. Kilpatrick, J. Swafford, & B. Findell (Eds.). Mathematics Learning Study Committee, Center for Education, Division for Behavioral and Social Sciences and Education. Washington, DC: National Academy Press.

National Research Council. (2001). *Eager to learn: Educating our preschoolers.* B. T. Bowman, M. S. Donovan, & M. S. Burns (Eds.). Committee on Early Childhood Pedagogy, Commission on Behavioral and Social Sciences and Education. Washington, DC: National Academy Press.

National Research Council and Institute of Medicine. (2000). *From neurons to neighborhoods: The science of early childhood development.* J. P. Shonkoff & D. A. Phillips (Eds.). Committee on Integrating the Science of Early Childhood Development, Board on Children, Youth, and Families, Commission on Behavioral and Social Sciences and Education. Washington, DC: National Academy Press.

National Urban League. (1998). *Learning science and math in your community.* National Parent Information Network. (http://npin.org/library/pre1998/n00283/n00283.html).

Patilla, P. (1999). *Math links series: Measuring.* Portsmouth, NH: Heinemann.

Payne, J. (Ed.). (1990). *Mathematics for the young child.* Reston, VA: National Council of Teachers of Mathematics.

Piaget, J., (1970). *The child's concept of number.* New York: Viking Press.

Piaget, J., & Inhelder, B. (1969). *The psychology of the child.* New York: Basic Books.

Polonsky, L. (Ed.). (2000). *Math for the very young: A handbook of activities for parents and teachers.* New York: John Wiley & Sons.

Richardson, K., & Salkeld, L. (1995). Transforming mathematics curriculum. In S. Bredekamp & T. Rosegrant (Eds.), *Reaching potentials: Transforming early childhood curriculum and assessment* (Vol. 2, pp. 23–42). Washington, DC: National Association for the Education of Young Children.

Seefeldt, C. (1993). Learning for freedom. *Young Children, 48,* 39–45.

Seefeldt, C. (1995). Art: A serious work. *Young Children, 50*(3), 39–54.

Seefeldt, C. (1997). *Social studies for the preschool–primary child.* Upper Saddle River, NJ: Merrill/Prentice-Hall.

Seefeldt, C., & Barbour, N. (1998). *Early childhood education: An introduction.* Upper Saddle River, NJ: Merrill/Prentice-Hall.

Seefeldt, C., & Galper, A. (2002). *Active experiences for active children—Science.* Upper Saddle River, NJ: Merrill/Prentice Hall.

Stanmark, J. K., Thompson, V., & Cossey, R. (1986). *Family math.* New York: Equals.

Vygotsky, L. (1978). *Thought and language.* Cambridge, MA: MIT Press.

Vygotsky, L. (1986). *Thought and language* (Rev. ed.). Cambridge, MA: The MIT Press.

Weaver, L. R., & Gaines, C. (1999). What to do when they don't speak English: Teaching mathematics to English-language learners in the early childhood classroom. In J. V. Copley (Ed.), *Mathematics in the early years* (pp. 198–204). Reston, VA: National Council of Teachers of Mathematics.

Wilson, R. A. (1995). Nature and young children: A natural connection. *Young Children, 50*(6), 4–7.

Wright, J. L., & Shade, D. (Eds.). (1994). *Young children: Active learners in a technological age.* Washington, DC: National Association for the Education of Young Children.

Youniss, J., & Damon, W. (1992). Social construction of Piaget's theory. In H. Beilin & P. B. Pufall (Eds.), *Piaget's theory: Perspectives and possibilities.* Hillsdale, NJ: Erlbaum.

Children's Books

Aardema, V. (1975). *Why mosquitoes buzz in people's ears.* New York: Dial Books for Young Readers.
Adler, D. A. (1999). *How tall, how short, how faraway.* New York: Holiday House.
Anno, M. (1987). *Anno's math games.* New York: Philomel Press.
Anno, M. (1999). *Anno's magic seeds.* New York: Paper Star.
Brown, M. W. (1947). *Goodnight moon/Buenas noches luna.* New York: Harper & Row.
Burns, M. (1994). *The greedy triangle.* New York: Scholastic.
Burns, M. (1996). *How many feet? How many tails?* New York: Scholastic Trade.
Carle, E. (1969). *The very hungry caterpillar.* London: Hamish Hamilton.
Carle, E. (1986). *The secret birthday message.* New York: Harper/Trophy.
Carle, E. (1996). *The grouchy ladybug.* Old Tappan, NJ: Scott Foresman (Pearson K–12).
Children's Television Workshop. (2000). *Cookie bakes up shapes.* New York: Preschool Press. Time-Life Books.
Dee, R. (1988). *Two ways to count to ten: A Liberian folktale.* New York: Henry Holt.
De Regniers, B. S. (1985). *So many cats!* Wilmington, MA: Houghton Mifflin.
Derubertis, B. (1999). *A collection for Kate.* New York: Kane Press.
Dodds, D. A. (1994). *The shape of things.* Cambridge, MA: Candlewick.
Ehlert, L. (2001). *Fish eyes: A book you can count on.* New York: Harcourt Brace.
Feelings, M. (1971). *Moja means one: Swahili counting book.* New York: Dial.
Fowler, R. (1993). *Ladybug on the move.* New York: Harcourt.
Fox, M. (1990). *Shoes from Grandpa.* London: A Division of Watts Publishing Group.
Gerth, M. (2001). *Ten little ladybugs.* New York: Piggy Toes Press.
Grifalconi, V. (1986). *The village of round and square houses.* Boston: Little Brown.
Grossman, V. (1999). *Ten little rabbits.* New York: Chronicle Books.
Grover, M. (1996). *Circles and squares everywhere.* New York: Harcourt.
Hirst, R. & S. (1990). *My place in space.* London: The Watts Publishing Group.
Hoban, T. (1985). *Is it larger? Is it smaller?* New York: Greenwillow Books.
Hoban, T. (1986). *Shapes, shapes, shapes.* New York: Greenwillow Books.
Hoban, T. (1987). *Dots, spots, speckles, and stripes.* New York: Greenwillow Books.
Hoban, T. (1996). *Circles, triangles, and squares.* New York: Greenwillow Books.
Hutchins, P. (1970). *Clocks and more clocks.* New York: Macmillan.
Hutchins, P. (1986). *The doorbell rang.* New York: Mulberry Books.
Hutchins, P. (1994). *Llaman a la puerta* (A. Marcuse, Trans.). New York: Mulberry Books/William Morrow.
Keats, J. E. (1990). *Over in the meadow.* New York: Puffin.

Keena, S., & Girouard, P. (1997). *More or less a mess.* New York: Cartwheel Books.

Keenan, S. (2001). *Lizzy's dizzy day, dizzy day.* New York: Cartwheel Books.

Martin, B., Jr., & Archambault, J. (1989). *Chicka chicka boom boom.* New York: Simon & Schuster Books for Young Readers.

Marvelous math: A book of poems. (1997). Selected by L. B. Hopkins. New York: Simon and Schuster Books for Young Readers.

McKissack, P. C. (1997). *Mirandy and brother wind.* New York: Alfred A. Knopf.

McMillan, B. (1986). *Becca backward, Becca forward: A book of concept pairs.* New York: HarperCollins.

Meeks, S. (2002). *Drip drop.* New York: HarperTrophy.

Murphy, S. (1997). *Betcha!* New York: HarperCollins.

Myller, R. (1991). *How big is a foot?* Old Tappan, NJ: Scott Foresman (Pearson K–12).

Reid, M. (1990). *The button box.* New York: Dutton.

Santomero, A. C. (1998). *The shape detectives.* New York: Simon Spotlight, an imprint of Simon and Schuster, Children's Publishing Division.

Say, A. (1982). *The bicycle man.* New York: Houghton Mifflin.

Serfozo, M. (1996). *There's a square: A book about shapes.* New York: Scholastic.

Seuss, Dr. (1988). *The shape of me and other stuff.* New York: Random House.

Shaw, C. G. (1988). *It looked like spilt milk.* New York: HarperTrophy.

Silverstein, S. (1976). *The missing piece.* New York: HarperCollins Children's Books.

Tompert, A. (1990). *Grandfather Tang's story.* New York: Crown.

Wing, R. W. (1963). *What is big?* New York: Holt, Rinehart and Winston.

Wood, J. (1992). *Moo, moo, brown cow.* New York: Gulliver Books.

Resources

Organizations and Web Sites

National Association for the Education of Young Children (NAEYC)
1509 16th Street NW
Washington, DC 20036
http://www.naeyc.org
Provides resources to members. You can download their recent position statement with the National Council of Teachers of Mathematics, entitled "Early Childhood Mathematics: Promoting Good Beginnings," at www.naeyc.org/resources/position_statements/psmath.htm.

National Council of Teachers of Mathematics (NCTM)
1906 Association Drive
Reston, VA 22091
http://nctm.org
Provides a large selection of educational materials and resources on-line. You can download all or a part of the principles and standards at http://standards.nctm.org/document. The standards are supported by "i-math online interactive, multimedia math investigations and e-math which are selected electronic examples from the electronic version of the principles and standards." There is nothing here for very young children, although some of the examples could be adapted.

National Council of Supervisors of Mathematics (NCSM)
http://www.ncsmonline.org
This Web site has a nice section of teaching resources beginning with kindergarten. There are science materials such as what manipulative to choose to teach what concept. This could be adapted for younger children.

U.S. Department of Education, Office of Educational Research and Improvement, National Institute on Early Childhood Development and Education
http://www.ed.gov/pubs/EarlyMath
This site has wonderful ideas for parents to help their children with math concepts in an everyday context. All of the activities are good and none are threatening. You can download a copy of their excellent math publication for parents and their 2-to 5-year-old children, *Where learning begins—Mathematics*. Teachers can easily use these ideas as well.

First-level Mathematics (KinderMath)
38 North Waterloo Road
Devon, PA 19333
1-610-687-6252

Equals and Family Math
Lawrence Hall of Science
University of California
Berkeley, CA 94720-5200
http://equals.lhs.berkeley.edu/
The EQUALS programs at the Lawrence Hall of Science, University of California at Berkeley, provide workshops and curriculum material in mathematics for teachers, parents, families, and community members. Their book *Family Math for Young Children: Comparing* is an excellent resource for teachers of children from Pre-K to grade 3.

National Parent Information Network Virtual Library
Learning Science and Math in Your Community
http://npin.org/library
Excellent resources for parents and the community. You can download "Learning Science and Math in Your Community," which is a publication of the National Urban League, Inc., 120 Wall St., New York, NY 10005.

National Head Start Association
1651 Prince Street
Alexandria, VA 22314
www.nhsa.org
Good resources in all curriculum areas for members of this organization.

Smithsonian—Folkway Recordings
750 9th Street NW Suite 4100
Washington, DC 20560
www.si.edu/folkways
Wonderful educational recordings—tapes and CDs—by Ella Jenkins, Hap Palmer, Rosemary Hallum, and others. There are many that deal with beginning math concepts, such as "Counting Games and Rhythms for the Little Ones" and "Dancing Numerals."

Educational Activities, Inc. K-3
P.O. Box 392
Freeport, NY 11520
www.edact.com
Some fine ideas for math activities for kindergarten and up. Some of them may be adapted for younger children.

Carol Hurst's Children's Literature Site
http://www.carolhurst.com
A very good Web site for locating excellent children's literature by curriculum area. The books are annotated. Many good fiction and nonfiction math books are listed by topic.

Math Forum at Drexel University
http://mathforum.org/
The forum features math resources by subject for K–12. You can also access Dr. Math, Teacher Exchange, and Key Issues in Math Education, among others.

Index

Aardema, V., 72
Abstract knowledge, 46, 87
Activities, experiences compared to, 4
Adding It Up (National Research Council), 53
Addition and subtraction of whole numbers, 77–78
Adler, D. A., 102, 108
Adults, 7, 9, 14. *See also* Parents; Teacher's role
Aesthetics, 17
Age appropriateness, 4, 6
Alexander, K. L., 6
Algebra concepts. *See also* Patterns and relationships
    addition and subtraction of whole numbers and, 77–78
    assessment and, 74, 84
    children's literature and, 72–73, 76, 77, 78
    experiences and, 75–79
    home-school connection and, 74, 80–82
    patterns and relationships and, 44, 70, 71, 75–76
    problem solving and, 129
    sorting, classifying, and ordering objects and, 70, 76–77
    as standard, 44, 70
    teacher's role and, 70–74
Ames, L. B., 41
Analysis. *See* Data description, organization, representation, and analysis
Andrews, A. G., 102
Anno, M., 59, 72, 78, 102, 104, 109, 129
Anno's Magic Seeds (Anno), 59, 129
Anno's Math Games (Anno), 72, 78, 102, 104, 109
Application of knowledge, 10, 11
Archambault, J., 73, 76
Art activities
    aesthetics and, 17
    continuity of learning and, 10, 18
    field trips and, 32, 33
    geometry and spatial awareness and, 17, 90, 92
    number and operation and, 63
    patterns and relationships and, 17, 24, 35, 76
Art centers, 19–20, 24
Assessment
    algebra concepts and, 74, 84
    authentic assessment, 43
    data description, organization, representation, and analysis, 118–119
    geometry and spatial awareness and, 89–90, 98
    measurement and, 104–105, 113
    number and operation and, 54–55
    problem solving and, 130
    teacher's role and, 26

Barber, J., 103
Barbour, N., 9, 11, 16, 17, 62, 77
Baroody, A. J., 52
Basile, C., 14, 30
Beauty, 17
Becca Backward, Becca, Forward (McMillan), 73
Bergman, L., 103
Berk, L. E., 26, 30
Betcha! (Murphy), 102
Bicycle Man, The (Say), 38
Biological sciences, 9–10
Bird areas, 23
Blaska, J. K., 20
Block areas
    counting and, 56–57
    geometry and spatial awareness and, 21, 22, 90, 92
    measurement and, 21, 22, 35
Books. *See* Children's literature; Library centers; Teacher's resources
Boston University-Chelsea Project for Mathematics, 18, 21
Bredekamp, S., 5, 6, 9, 17, 41, 46
Bronfenbrenner, U., 30
Bronson, M. B., 18, 21
Brown, M. W., 73, 76
Bruner, J., 7, 10
Burns, M., 87, 93, 102, 129
Burts, D. C., 6
Businesses, 35
Button Box, The (Reid), 73, 78

Calendars, 60, 76, 100, 103, 107
Calomiris, Z., 19
Cardinality, 53
Carle, E., 87, 102, 107
Cavanagh, M., 72, 87
Centers. *See also specific centers and areas*
    children's literature and, 9
    development of mathematical thinking and, 14
    indoor spaces and, 18–23
    initiative and, 5
    outdoor spaces and, 23–25

Central tendency, 126
Charlesworth, R., 6, 102, 121
Checklists, 11
Chicka Chicka Boom Boom (Martin and Archambault), 73, 76
Children's knowledge, 40–41, 44–45
Children's literature
   algebra concepts and, 72–73, 76, 77, 78
   book and library centers, 20–21
   centers and, 9
   checklist for choosing math books, 47, 114
   concepts and, 18, 20
   data description, organization, representation, and analysis and, 117
   experiences and, 9, 45–46
   field trip experiences and, 32, 33
   geometry and spatial awareness and, 87–88, 90–92, 93
   home-school connection and, 37
   measurement and, 102–103, 107, 108–109
   names of numerals and, 59
   number and operation and, 53–54, 59–60
   problem solving and, 129
   Spanish-language books, 36–37
Children's self-evaluations, 10, 11, 74, 90, 104
Children's Television Workshop, 87, 91
Choices, 5-6, 14, 24
Circles, Triangles, and Squares (Hoban), 88, 91
Circles and Squares Everywhere (Grover), 88
Classifying objects. *See* Sorting, classifying, and ordering objects
Classroom pets, 15, 107–108
Classroom supplies
   for algebra concepts, 73
   for geometry and spatial awareness, 88–89
   for measurement, 103
   for number and operation, 54
Clements, D. H., 22, 116
Clocks and More Clocks (Hutchins), 102
Cognitive development, 16, 40–41
Collection for Kate, A (Derubertis), 117, 119
Collections, 116, 119–120, 128
Commune di Reggio Emilia, 10
Communication, 10, 11, 70, 74
Community, 8, 30, 32, 33–36
Comparing/contrasting skills
   block areas and, 22
   experiences and, 5, 134–135
   garden areas and, 24
   outdoor spaces and, 31
   school building and, 31
   woodworking centers and, 20
Computer stations, 22, 46, 93
Concepts
   aesthetics and, 17
   algebra concepts and, 71

   block areas and, 21–22
   children's literature and, 18, 20
   counting and, 52–53
   data description, organization, representation, and analysis, 116
   development of, 40–41, 52
   geometry and spatial awareness and, 86
   indoor spaces and, 18, 20, 21–22
   learning environments and, 14
   meaning and, 7
   measurement and, 100–101
   number and operation and, 52–53, 64
   outdoor spaces and, 23, 24, 25, 30
   problem solving and, 128–129
   sociodramatic play areas and, 21
   teacher's role and, 26
Conservation (Piaget's theory), 41
Content
   expanding experiences and, 40, 45–46
   integrity and meaning and, 4, 7
   knowledge of children and, 40–41, 44–45
   knowledge of mathematics and, 42–43
   standards and, 43–44, 90, 105
Continuity of learning, 4, 9–10, 18
Cookie Bakes Up Shapes (Children's Television Workshop), 87, 91
Copley, J. V., 52, 53, 70, 119
Copple, C., 6, 41
Cossey, R., 53, 118
Counting
   experiences and, 5, 55–64
   field trips and, 35
   garden areas and, 24
   graphs and, 125
   music areas and, 22
   outdoor spaces and, 24, 31
   problem solving and, 129
   school building and, 31
   standards and, 43
   teacher's role and, 52–55
Count on Math (Schiller and Peterson), 72
Curriculum
   algebra concepts and, 71, 74
   assessment and, 43
   children's literature and, 18
   concepts and, 7
   continuity of learning and, 10
   counting and, 52
   field trips and, 33, 35
   home-school connection and, 37
   interaction and, 8
   measurement and, 105
   neighborhood resources and, 36
   number and operation and, 64
   problem solving and, 14
   standards and, 42
   teacher's role and, 11, 25

Dacey, L., 72, 87
Damon, W., 30
Dance, 10, 92
Data description, organization, representation, and analysis
    assessment and, 118–119
    block areas and, 21
    experiences and, 119–125
    field trips and, 33
    home-school connection and, 117–118, 125
    outdoor spaces and, 23
    problem solving and, 128–129
    reflection and, 126
    as standard, 44
    teacher's role and, 116–119
Davila Coates, G., 36, 38
Decision making, 5–6, 14
Dee, R., 73, 77
DeLoache, J. S., 8
Democratic society, 6, 8
De Regniers, B. S., 73
Derubertis, B., 117, 119
Description. *See* Data description, organization, representation, and analysis
Developmentally Appropriate Practice in Early Childhood Programs (Bredekamp and Copple), 41
Dewey, J., 4, 6, 8, 9, 10, 11, 27, 30, 40
DeWolf, M., 6
Dighe, J., 19
Documenting children's learning
    algebra concepts and, 79
    data description, organization, representation, and analysis, 126
    geometry and spatial awareness and, 94
    measurement and, 109
    number and operation and, 64
    problem solving and, 136
Dodds, D. A., 87
Doorbell Rang, The (Hutchins), 36–37, 73, 77
Dots, Spots, Speckles, and Stripes (Hoban), 73, 76
Dramatic play. *See* Sociodramatic play
Drip Drop (Meeks), 102
Dyson, A. H., 8

Early Childhood (U.S. Department of Education), 74, 89
Earth sciences, 10
Education, U.S. Department of, 74, 89, 103
Ehlert, L., 53, 59
Entwisle, D. R., 6
Equity, 42
Estimating skills, 22, 24, 31, 33, 35
Evaluation of children. *See also* Children's self-evaluations
    algebra concepts and, 74, 84
    data description, organization, representation, and analysis, 118–119
    geometry and spatial awareness and, 89–90, 98
    measurement and, 104–105, 113
    number and operation and, 54–55
    problem solving and, 130
Experiences
    activities compared to, 4
    algebra concepts and, 75–79
    community and, 30, 32
    content and, 40, 45–46
    continuity of learning and, 4, 9–10
    data description, organization, representation, and analysis, 119–125
    field trips and, 32–33
    geometry and spatial awareness and, 90–92
    home-school connection and, 30, 36–38
    interaction and, 4, 7–9
    language and, 4, 9
    meaning and, 4–7, 30
    measurement and, 5, 105–109
    neighborhood and, 30, 32, 33–36
    number and operation and, 55–64
    problem solving and, 130–136
    reflection and, 4, 10–11
Experiences in Math for Young Children (Charlesworth), 102
Experiential learning, 9

Family. *See* Home-school connection; Parents
Family Math Nights, 37
Family Math program, 36–37, 103
Family Math (Stanmark, Thompson, and Cossey), 53, 118
Feelings, Muriel, 37
Field trips
    geometry and spatial awareness and, 32, 86
    guidelines for, 32–33
    health and safety tips for, 34
    language and, 9
    neighborhood as mathematics laboratory and, 34–35
    symbolic thought and, 77
Findell, C. R., 72, 87
Firsthand experiences, 4, 5, 40. *See also* Experiences
Fish Eyes (Ehlert), 53, 59
Flynn, L. L., 15, 16, 17
Fowler, R., 102
Fox, M., 73
Franco, Betsy, 78

Gainer, Cindy, 72
Gaines, C., 38
Galper, A., 15, 16, 55
Garden areas, 23–24, 59, 108
Geist, E., 33
Gender, 36

Geometry and spatial awareness
    art activities and, 17, 90, 92
    assessment and, 89–90, 98
    block areas and, 21, 22, 90, 92
    children's literature and, 87–88, 90–92, 93
    experiences for, 90–92
    field trips and, 32, 86
    home-school connection and, 89, 95–96
    knowledge of mathematics and, 43
    observation of children and, 89, 97
    outdoor spaces and, 24
    problem solving and, 89, 93, 129
    school building and, 31
    teacher's role and, 86–90
    woodworking centers and, 20
Geometry from Africa (Gerdes), 87
Gerdes, P., 87
Gerth, M., 53, 59
Gesell, A., 41
Girouard, P., 117
Goals and objectives
    algebra concepts and, 71
    data description, organization, representation, and analysis, 116–117
    geometry and spatial awareness and, 86–87
    measurement and, 101
    number and operation and, 53
    problem solving and, 129
Goodnight Moon (Brown), 73, 76
Grandfather Tang's Story (Tompert), 93
Graphs
    data description, organization, representation, and analysis and, 116
    experiences and, 121–125
    field trips and, 32
    home-school connection and, 117, 118
    observation of children and, 118–119
    problem solving and, 128, 129
    school building and, 31
Great Graphing (Martin and Miller), 117
Greedy Triangle, The (Burns), 87, 93
Greenes, C., 14, 18
Greenes, Carol, 72
Greenes, C. E., 87
Grifalconi, V., 87
Grossman, V., 53, 59, 64
Grouch Ladybug, The (Carle), 102, 107
Group work and projects
    algebra concepts and, 74
    geometry and spatial awareness and, 89
    interaction and, 8
    learning environments and, 14, 16–17
    measurement and, 104
    problem solving and, 130–136
Grover, M., 88

Hallum, Rosemary, 92
Hart, C. H., 6
Health and safety, 15, 25, 34, 106
Hearing impairments, 16
Hirst, R., 88, 91
Hirst, S., 88, 91
Hoban, T., 73, 76, 88, 91, 102
Home-school connection
    algebra concepts and, 74, 80–82
    book and library centers and, 20
    continuity of learning and, 10
    data description, organization, representation, and analysis and, 117–118, 125
    experiences and, 30, 36–38
    geometry and spatial awareness and, 89, 95–96
    learning environments and, 17
    measurement and, 103–104, 110–111
    number and operation and, 54, 65–68
    problem solving and, 74, 129, 137–138
    school building and outdoor environment, 31
    sociodramatic play areas and, 21
Hopkins, L. B., 73, 78, 102
Housekeeping center, 9, 21, 60
How Big Is a Foot? (Myller), 102
How Many Feet? How Many Tails? (Burns), 129
How Much is a Million? (Schwartz), 102, 107
How Tall, How Short, How Faraway (Adler), 102, 108
Hutchins, P., 36–37, 73, 77, 102

Ilg, F. L., 41
Imagination, 11
Incidental learnings, 35, 70, 86
Inclusion
    field trip experiences and, 32
    learning environments and, 15–17
Indoor spaces
    art centers, 19–20
    block areas, 21–22
    book and library centers, 20–21
    computer stations, 22
    integration of, 18
    math or manipulatives areas, 18–19
    music areas, 22
    quiet spaces, 23
    science areas, 19
    sociodramatic play areas, 21
    water and sand areas, 22
    woodworking centers, 20
Infant and Child in the Culture of Today (Gesell, Ilg, and Ames), 41
Inhelder, B., 5, 8, 128
Initiative, 4, 5–6, 14
Integrity, 4, 7
Interaction
    centers and, 14
    experiences and, 4, 7–9
    outdoor spaces and, 24
    teacher's role and, 9, 14, 26
Is It Larger? Is It Smaller? (Hoban), 102
It Looked Like Spilt Milk (Shaw), 103

Index

Jenkins, Ella, 76, 78
Johnson-Foote, B., 58

Katz, L., 10, 26
Keats, E. J.., 54, 59
Keena, S., 117
Keenan, S., 129
Kieff, J., 15, 16, 17
Kim, S. L., 22
Knowledge construction, 5, 42
Kohl, Mary Ann, 72

Labels, 120–121
Ladybug on the Move (Fowler), 102
Language
    algebra concepts and, 79
    data description, organization, representation, and analysis and, 116
    experiences and, 4, 9
    geometry and spatial awareness and, 86, 90, 91, 93
    interaction and, 7
    language of mathematics, 7, 46, 86
    learning environments and, 14
    measurement and, 108
    outdoor spaces and, 24
    preoperational thinking and, 41
    Spanish-language books, 36–37
    teacher's role and, 26
Learning environments
    design of, 14
    essentials of, 15–17
    indoor spaces and, 18–23
    outdoor spaces and, 23–25
Let's Do Math, 129
Library centers, 20–21
Listening, 9, 14
Little Kids, Powerful Problem Solvers (Andrews and Trafton), 102
Lizzy's Dizzy Day, Dizzy Day (Keenan), 129
Loughlin, C., 16
Lynch, E. C., 20

Mallory, B. L., 16–17, 17
Maps
    geometry and spatial awareness and, 87, 90, 92, 93
    neighborhood resources and, 35
    sand areas and, 22
    school building and, 31
Marcon, R., 6
Martin, B., Jr., 73, 76
Martin, L., 117
Marvelous Math (Hopkins), 73, 78, 102, 108
Maryland State Department of Education, 7
Marzoff, D. P., 8
Math Arts (Kohn and Gainer), 72
Math backpack, 38
Math Curse (Scieszka and Smith), 108–109
Mathematics and Literature (Burns), 102
Mathematics for the Young Child (Payne), 71, 102
Math for the Very Young (Polonsky), 117
Math journals
    algebra concepts and, 74, 75, 78, 79
    geometry and spatial awareness and, 90
    measurement and, 103, 104
    problem solving and, 135–136
Math Links Series (Patilla), 102
Math Night Out, 117
Math or manipulatives areas, 18–19, 24, 56
Matthias, Margaret, 72
McCracken, Janet, 54
McKissack, Patricia C., 78
McMillan, B., 73
Mean, 126
Meaning
    centers and, 14
    counting and, 58
    experiences and, 4–7, 30
    graphs and, 125
Measurement
    art activities and, 17
    assessment and, 104–105, 113
    block areas and, 21, 22, 35
    children's literature and, 102–103, 107, 108–109
    experiences and, 5, 105–109
    field trips and, 33, 35
    garden areas and, 24
    home-school connection and, 103–104, 110–111
    observation of children and, 104, 112
    outdoor areas and, 23, 31
    problem solving and, 108–109, 129
    school building and, 31
    as standard, 44, 100, 105
    teacher's role and, 100–105
    woodworking centers and, 20
Meeks, S., 102
Miller, M., 117
Mirandy and Brother Wind (McKissack), 78
Missing Piece, The (Silverstein), 88, 93
Mode, 126
Moja Means One (Feelings), 37
Moo, Moo, Brown Cow (Wood), 54, 59
More or Less a Mess (Keena and Girouard), 117
More Than 1, 2, 3– (McCracken), 54
Multicultural Game Book, The (Orlando), 87
Murphy, S., 102
Museums, 30, 32, 35–36
Music activities
    continuity of learning and, 10, 18
    one-to-one correspondence and, 61
    patterns and relationships and, 76, 78
Music areas, 22
Myller, R., 102
My Place in Space (Hirst and Hirst), 88, 91

Names of numerals, 46, 52, 53, 58–60, 125
National Association for the Education of Young Children, 4, 5, 20, 36, 40, 42, 43, 44, 54, 71
National Council of Teachers of Mathematics, 4, 5, 6, 7, 18, 20, 21, 25, 26, 30, 36, 40, 42, 43, 44, 55, 56, 61, 71, 86, 87, 90, 93, 100, 101, 105, 129, 136
National Research Council, 5, 6, 52, 53, 58, 62, 116
National Urban League, 33, 35
Navigating Through Algebra in Prekindergarten-Grade 2 (Greenes, Cavanagh, Dacey, Findell, and Small), 72
Navigating Through Geometry in Prekindergarten-Grade 2 (Findell, Small, Cavanagh, Dacey, Greenes, and Shellfield), 87
Neighborhood, 30, 32, 33–36
New, R. S., 17
Newsletters, 37, 54, 89, 103, 118
Number and operation
    assessment and, 54–55
    block areas and, 21
    children's daily use of, 62–63
    children's literature and, 53–54, 59–60
    computer stations and, 22
    experiences for, 55–64
    home-school connection and, 54, 65–68
    knowledge of mathematics and, 43
    problem solving and, 46, 62, 129
    teacher's role and, 52–55, 62

Object permanence, 41
Observation of children
    algebra concepts and, 74, 83
    data description, organization, representation, and analysis, 118–119
    geometry and spatial awareness and, 89, 97
    home-school connection and, 37
    measurement and, 104, 112
    number and operation and, 55
    problem solving and, 130
    teacher's role and, 26
Observation skills, 5, 22, 24, 33, 133–134
O'Neill, Mary, 108
One-to-one correspondence, 52, 53, 61–62, 125
Ordering objects. *See* Sorting, classifying, and ordering objects
Organization. *See also* Data description, organization, representation, and analysis
    algebra concepts and, 78
    art centers and, 19
    reflection and, 10, 11
    as standard, 44
Orlando, L., 87
Otis, Rebecca, 72
Otis Hurst, Carol, 72
Outdoor spaces
    art spaces, 24
    context and, 30

data description, organization, representation, and analysis and, 116
health and safety and, 16
home-school connection and, 31
math/science and nature discovery areas, 23–25
math spaces, 24
measurement and, 106
physical spaces, 24–25
Over in the Meadow (Keats), 54, 59

Palmer, Hap, 78
Parents. *See also* Home-school connection
    book and library centers and, 20
    content of mathematics and, 45
    continuity of learning and, 10
    data description, organization, representation, and analysis and, 118
    field trip experiences and, 33, 34
    geometry and spatial awareness and, 89, 91, 93
    health and safety and, 15
    involvement of, 36
    measurement and, 103–104, 109, 110–111
    as neighborhood resources, 36
    number and operation and, 54
    questioning skills and, 37, 74
    sociodramatic play areas and, 21
Parizeau, N., 103
Patilla, P., 102
Patterns and relationships
    algebra concepts and, 44, 70, 71, 75–76
    art activities and, 17, 24, 35, 76
    art spaces and, 24
    block areas and, 21
    computer stations and, 22
    experiences and, 5
    field trips and, 32
    garden areas and, 24
    generalizations about, 75
    home-school connection and, 74
    music activities and, 76, 78
    music areas and, 22
    outdoor spaces and, 31
    primary grades and, 78
    as standard, 44
Payne, J., 102
Payne, Joseph N., 71
Peer interaction, 7, 14
Peterson, Lynne, 72
Physical activities, 76, 92
Physical sciences, 10
Physical spaces, 24–25
Piaget, J., 5, 8, 30, 40–41, 42, 46, 55, 128
Picturing Math (Otis Hurst and Otis), 72
Play, and interaction, 7–8
Polonsky, L., 117
Portfolios
    algebra concepts and, 74
    geometry and spatial relations and, 90

measurement and, 104
reflection and, 11
Potential developmental level, 45
Preconcepts, 41
Predicting outcomes, 22, 75, 79, 132–133
Preoperational stage, 41
Presentations, 10, 11
Primary grades
   algebra concepts and, 78–79
   continuity of learning and, 10
   data description, organization, representation, and analysis, 126
   geometry and spatial awareness and, 93
   measurement and, 108–109
   number and operation and, 64
   problem solving and, 136
Principles and Standards for School Mathematics (National Council of Teachers of Mathematics), 90, 105
Probability, 126
Problem solving
   assessment and, 130
   curriculum and, 14
   experiences and, 130–136
   geometry and spatial awareness and, 89, 93, 129
   home-school connection and, 74, 129, 137–138
   initiative and, 5–6
   knowledge of mathematics and, 43, 70
   measurement and, 108–109, 129
   number and operation and, 46, 62, 129
   patterns and relationships and, 75
   as standard, 44, 136
   teacher's role and, 26, 128–130

Questioning skills
   outdoor spaces and, 23
   parents and, 37, 74
   problem solving and, 130, 131–132
   teacher's role and, 26, 46, 131
Quiet spaces, 23, 25

Radeloff, D. J., 121
Raw materials, 6
Read Any Good Math Lately? (Whitin and Wilde), 87
Reading, 9, 14, 20–21
Reflection
   algebra concepts and, 78
   art centers and, 19
   choices and, 6
   data description, organization, representation, and analysis, 126
   experiences and, 4, 10–11
   field trip experiences and, 33, 35
   geometry and spatial awareness and, 92–93
   number and operation and, 63–64
   problem solving and, 128, 135–136
Reggio Emilia, Italy, 10, 11, 17, 20
Reid, M., 73, 78

Representation. *See* Data description, organization, representation, and analysis
Richardson, K., 75
Right Stuff for Children Birth to 8, The (Bronson), 18
Rosegrant, T., 9, 46

Safety, 15, 25, 34, 106
Salkeld, L., 75
Sand areas
   counting and, 57
   indoor spaces and, 22
   measurement and, 103, 107
   outdoor spaces and, 23
Santomero, A. C., 88, 90–91
Say, Allen, 38
Scale, 120–121
Schiller, Pam, 72
School building, 31
Schwartz, D. A., 102, 107
Science areas, 18, 19
Sciences, 9–10, 18, 24
Scieszka, Jon, 108–109
Secret Birthday Message, The (Carle), 87
Seefeldt, C., 6, 7, 9, 11, 15, 16, 17, 32, 55, 62, 77
Sefozo, M., 88
Semilogical thinking, 41
Senses, 16
Sensorimotor stage, 40–41
Sequential counting, 5, 53, 60–61
Seuss, Dr., 88, 92
Shade, D., 22
Shape Detectives, The (Santomero), 88, 90–91
Shape of Me and Other Stuff, The (Seuss), 88, 92
Shape of Things, The (Dodds), 87
Shapes, Shapes, Shapes (Hoban), 73, 88, 91
Shaw, C. G., 103
Shellfield, L. J., 87
Shoes from Grandpa (Fox), 73
Silverstein, S., 88, 93
Small, M., 72, 87
Smith, Jacquelin, 72
Smith, Lane, 108–109
Social knowledge, 46
Social studies, 10, 18
Sociodramatic play
   counting and, 56, 57
   field trip experiences and, 32, 33
   geometry and spatial awareness and, 90
   interaction and, 7–8
   learning environments and, 21
So Many Cats! (De Regniers), 73
Sorting, classifying, and ordering objects
   algebra concepts and, 70, 76–77
   block areas and, 22
   experiences and, 5
   geometry and spatial awareness and, 93
   home-school connection and, 74

Sorting, classifying, and ordering objects—*continued*
  music areas and, 22
  organization and, 11
  outdoor spaces and, 24, 31
  primary grades and, 78–79
  woodworking centers and, 20
Spanish-language books, 36–37
Spark Your Child's Success in Math and Science (Barber, Parizeau, and Bergman), 103
Speaking, 9
Standards
  algebra concepts and, 44, 70
  block areas and, 21
  content and, 43–44, 90, 105
  geometry and spatial awareness and, 87, 90
  list of, 43–44
  measurement and, 44, 100, 105
  principles for teaching mathematics and, 42–43
  problem solving and, 44, 136
Stanmark, J. K., 53, 118
Structured interviews
  algebra concepts and, 74
  data description, organization, representation, and analysis, 118
  geometry and spatial awareness and, 90
  measurement and, 104
  number and operation and, 55
  problem solving and, 130
Success/failure, 6, 14, 40
Suina, J., 16
Symbolic thought
  algebra concepts and, 70, 74, 77–78, 79
  sensorimotor stage and, 41
  sociodramatic play and, 8

Teacher's resources
  algebra concepts and, 71–72
  for cognitive development, 41
  for data description, organization, representation, and analysis, 117
  geometry and spatial awareness and, 87
  for measurement, 102
  for number and operation, 53
  problem solving and, 129
Teacher's role
  algebra concepts and, 70–74
  assessment and, 26
  content of mathematics and, 44–45
  data description, organization, representation, and analysis, 116–119
  expanding experiences and, 40, 45–46
  interaction and, 9, 14, 26
  learning environments and, 14, 25–26
  number and operation and, 52–55, 62
  problem solving and, 26, 128–130
  questioning skills and, 26, 46, 131
  reflection and, 11
  in teaching mathematics, 42

  woodworking centers and, 20
Technology, role of, 42
Ten Little Ladybugs (Gerth), 53, 59
Ten Little Rabbits (Grossman), 53, 59, 64
There's a Square (Serfozo), 88
Thiessen, Diane, 72
Thompson, V., 36, 38, 53, 118
Time concepts, 100, 104, 107
To Make a Portrait of a Lion (Commune di Reggio Emilia), 10
Tompert, A., 93
Tools
  health and safety and, 15
  home-school connection and, 38
  measurement and, 100, 105
  outdoor spaces and, 23, 25
  school building and, 31
  science areas and, 19
  woodworking centers and, 20
Trafton, P. R., 102
Two Ways to Count to Ten (Dee), 73, 77

Van Zutphen, C., 19
Very Hungry Caterpillar, The (Carle), 102, 107
Village of Round and Square Houses, The (Grifalconi), 87
Visual arts, 10
Visual impairments, 16
Vygotsky, L., 5, 8, 9, 26, 30, 45

Water areas
  counting and, 57
  indoor spaces and, 22
  measurement and, 103, 107
  outdoor spaces and, 23
Weaver, L. R., 38
What Is Big? (Wing), 103
Whitin, D. J., 87
Why Mosquitoes Buzz in People's Ears (Aardema), 72
Wigfield, A., 55
Wilde, S., 87
Wilkins, J. L. M., 52
Wilson, R. A., 17
Wing, R. W., 103
Winsler, A., 26, 30
Wonderful World of Mathematics (Thiessen, Matthias, and Smith), 72
Wood, J., 54, 59
Woodworking centers, 20
Wright, J. L., 22
Writing, 9, 14, 60

Young Child and Mathematics, The (Copley), 53
Youniss, J., 30

Zone of proximal development, 5, 9, 26, 45